MANAGING EMPLOYEE TURNOVER

MANAGING EMPLOYEE TURNOVER

A POSITIVE APPROACH

Edward Roseman

A DIVISION OF AMERICAN MANAGEMENT ASSOCIATIONS

Dedicated to my wife and jogging partner, who listened as this book emerged during our morning runs.

Library of Congress Cataloging in Publication Data

Roseman, Edward.
   Managing employee turnover.

   Includes index.
    1. Labor turnover.   2. Personnel management.
I. Title.
HF5549.5.T8R57   658.3'14   80-69690
ISBN 0-8144-5585-9

FIRST PRINTING

Preface

PEOPLE leave organizations. They leave because their performance was not satisfactory, or management didn't like them, or management felt they did not "fit it." Often, particularly within an increasingly mobile workforce, people leave hoping to find a "better job."

This job exodus—*turnover*—affects all managers, either directly or indirectly. It is costly and disruptive and may be symptomatic of serious, unresolved organizational deficiencies.

In studying turnover in different organizations, I have heard several common themes:

"Eleanor could not have left at a worse time. We were facing the end-of-the-month closing, and nobody in the department knew how to do her job. By the time a replacement was trained and functioning, we were getting 'heat' from everybody. No matter how much overtime the other members of the staff and I put in, we couldn't get ahead of the workload. And working under that pressure contributed to embarrassing problems."

"Sam burns out subordinates. Either he fires them or they quit faster than they can be replaced. The company's recruiters feel that they are working for him full time. The only ones who aren't complaining are the outside search firms. They're making a fortune keeping him supplied with applicants."

"I sometimes think we are the training ground for our competitors. We find people with good potential, develop their skills, and give them needed experience. Then, before we can get a full return on our investment, we lose them to our competition. What are we doing wrong?"

It's possible that no one is doing anything wrong. The turnover may be inevitable and unavoidable. However, in my experience, I have uncovered a considerable amount of turnover—voluntary and involuntary—that is controllable through modest corrective and preventive programs.

You may nod in agreement, but at the same time you may say:

"I know what has to be done. I just can't get it done in our organization. It will take a heavy commitment of staff, time, and money. Management just won't give a full corporate program its blessing unless the organization is facing an out-of-control turnover problem.

"The organization's overall turnover statistics just aren't dramatic enough to make management insecure. Yet I know that we already have serious problems within individual work units, and other problems elsewhere are becoming serious."

Usually, turnover problems do not reach the critical stage, requiring a top management mandate and organizationwide attention. Instead, serious turnover problems develop in subunits of an organization and are obscured by the total organization's statistics. Like a scene in an old Humphrey Bogart movie, the mobster instructs his enforcer to "work him over good, but don't touch his face. I don't want the big boss to know what happened to him."

Organizations get "worked over good," and the "big boss" never knows what happened. Human resources are continually wasted, seriously damaging organizational effectiveness, yet turnover statistics remain at an acceptable level.

For example, one large organization I know well rarely exceeds 1½ percent annual turnover. Compared with other companies in the same industry, it has an enviable turnover record. Yet turnover is virtually out of control in several of its major divisions. Even more important, in critical job functions the company has had extraordinary turnover statistics. Management explains away the "special cases" of turnover:

"Everybody wants good minority employees. You can't expect to keep them more than two or three years."

"Salesmen just don't stay on the job. They're not stable employees."

"Engineers are in such demand now that they can get jobs at will, making much more money with each move."

The focus of this book is on the average line manager and his or her responsibility in controlling turnover—voluntary and involuntary. The book does not advocate heroic, staff-administered corporate programs requiring heavy commitments of time and money. Rather, it emphasizes *commonsense actions* that can have considerable impact on controlling turnover. I feel the line manager is in the best position to intervene in the process early, confronting turnover before it gets out of control.

If every manager in the organization could save a single employee each year, the impact on the organization would be enormous. And since an individual manager may have an opportunity to save more than one employee in a year, the potential benefits certainly merit the company's full attention.

Unfortunately, line managers are not always willing to confront turnover. They see it as someone else's problem and abdicate their responsibility to personnel staff. They don't understand the fundamental issues and problems. And they don't realize that they are in a unique position to take positive action.

This book is intended as a commonsense action handbook for managers. Part One explores fundamental issues answering such vital questions as:

o How much turnover is too much?
o What are the critical differences between people who stay with an organization and people who leave?
o Which kind of turnover is more acceptable—forced or voluntary?
o Why do people leave organizations?
o What are the real costs of turnover?

Part Two discusses underlying problems created by managers that lead to turnover. By the way they select people, assign work, offer rewards, supervise, and build a work environment, managers can have substantial impact on turnover.

Part Three suggests ways to establish an early-warning system to diagnose the potential for turnover within an organization. The opportunity to confront turnover successfully is much greater when underlying problems are recognized early.

Part Four presents ways to retain valued employees. It shows managers how to develop a retention strategy, how to counsel potential leavers, and how to soften the impact of unexpected turnover by using human resources planning techniques.

Part Five provides guidelines for improving interpersonal skills. Since the burden of confronting turnover falls primarily on first-line managers, it is critical that they strengthen their ability to initiate constructive one-to-one dialogues with troubled employees.

Part Six examines recent social changes and their impact on turnover in the future. These changes include second careers, the new occupational role of women, working couples, the extended retirement age, the increasing educational level of the workforce, and changes in attitude about the quality of work life.

Throughout the book practical, commonsense actions are suggested to help managers retain valued employees.

Anyone responsible for the supervision of others can't afford to be a spectator, hoping that employees will stay with the organization and remain content and productive. Instead, managers must accept responsibility for confronting turnover and develop a retention strategy.

Edward Roseman

Contents

PART ONE

FUNDAMENTAL

ISSUES

Before managers can confront turnover, they must understand several fundamental issues:

- Turnover has both good and bad aspects. Sometimes it is necessary and unavoidable; at other times it is avoidable, controllable, and wasteful of resources.
- Managers' tendency to be concerned only with voluntary turnover ("quits") and to whitewash involuntary turnover ("dismissals") can lead to serious problems.
- Some people withdraw from the company by leaving; others withdraw by staying. By studying the "leavers" and the "stayers," managers can better understand turnover.
- Turnover is the final event in a complex process that begins when an employee is hired. It is characterized by "trigger" events, some of which represent managerial missteps.
- All turnover—voluntary and involuntary, desirable and undesirable—incurs costs, both economic and social. It is the manager's responsibility to try to minimize these costs.

CHAPTER 1

Turnover: Good or Bad?

TURNOVER is not a numbers game. Sometimes, the only thing companies do about turnover is maintain a complex reporting system. However, statistics don't tell the whole story. To illustrate, let's compare two companies with a very acceptable turnover rate of 1½ percent per year:

Company A is a large manufacturing organization with major plants at several locations across the country. Because of a change in top management, and the resultant change in policies and procedures, in the last year the company has lost a large number of experienced, long-term employees with highly specialized skills.

Company B is a smaller, nonmanufacturing business operating out of one primary site in a very desirable location. Its turnover rate over the years has been consistent and primarily represents the movement of short-term, unskilled clerical workers. The turnover is predictable and rarely has any impact on the smooth running of operations.

Obviously, Company A has a much more serious turnover problem than Company B. Yet both companies take pride in their *low* turnover rate.

TURNOVER STATISTICS

Turnover comparisons can be misleading, since company conditions vary greatly. As you can see in Figure 1, the size of an organization, the nature of its business, and its geographical location are just some of the factors that contribute to variations in turnover rate.

To make the reporting of turnover statistics even more confusing, there are basic definitional differences. A primary issue is the extent to which turnover is controllable. Retirement, illness, death, pregnancy, and reductions in staff because of economic conditions are uncontrollable factors that should be segregated from controllable "quits" and "dismissals." Voluntary and involuntary turnover statistics should also be segregated. However, these often are not clearly differentiated. For example:

A talented accountant with an irritating personality was passed over for promotion, repeatedly denied merit salary increases, given no recognition, and treated with coolness by the departmental manager and his peers. Eventually, he "got the message" and resigned. Was this a resignation or an involuntary termination?

A brilliant sales representative, educated as a teacher, discovered after six months of selling experience that

Figure 1. Average turnover rates, first nine months of 1978.

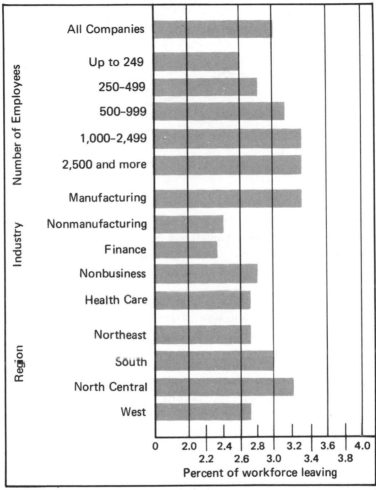

Source: Bureau of National Affairs, *Quarterly Report on Absences and Turnover*, 1978. Reproduced with permission.

the job just wasn't "right" for her. She had performed well in her training class and was still too new in the sales territory to be accountable for her performance. Yet she knew that she had begun to fail at the job. She surprised her manager by announcing her resignation. Was this a voluntary or involuntary termination?

Figure 2. Survival curve.

Length of Service (months)

Turnover statistics become even more confusing when we consider the many variations in reporting. Some organizations rely primarily on a simple *labor turnover rate* (LTR), which relates the number of leavers to the average number employed:

$$\text{LTR} = \frac{\text{Number of leavers} \times 100}{\text{Average number in employment} \times 100}$$

In addition to a gross labor turnover rate, some companies construct survival curves, tracking the percentage of survivors after varying lengths of service. (See Figure 2.) This kind of reporting focuses attention on how weaknesses in selection methods can create early turnover problems.

Another data collection method is the frequency distribution. Figure 3, a frequency distribution of "stayers,"

Figure 3. Frequency distribution of "stayers."

Years in Job	Number	Percent
Under 1 year	10	25.0
1–2 years	20	50.0
2–5 years	5	12.5
Over 5 years	5	12.5
Total	40	100.0

helps to pinpoint the time periods when employees are most vulnerable to separation.

The method a company uses to report turnover may hide or highlight the problem. Thus proper reporting is a primary consideration in determining whether a company has "good" or "bad" turnover.

BENEFITS OF TURNOVER

The movement of employees in and out of an organization gives it vitality. Ideally, people with fresh ideas, different frames of reference, and unique experiences are continually joining the organization. And employees who don't fit in well—because of deficiencies in skills, temperament, energy, or drive—leave the organization. As less qualified people leave, openings are created for more qualified replacements. When this process functions well, the organization is continually revitalized and upgraded.

Certainly, turnover is an ideal way to deal with "problem" employees. Termination rids the organization of malcontents and troublemakers. It helps to break up informal organizational groups that waste time and resist change.

Another important benefit of turnover is that it encourages management to reexamine the organizational structure and the content of jobs. Sometimes, the impetus for change comes from the loss of valued employees.

Turnover can also have significant financial benefits. High-priced talent may be traded for lower-priced talent with equal capabilities. As employees move past the midpoint of their salary ranges, pay rewards often outstrip increases in productivity. And the longer employees stay with a company, the more they accumulate vested interests in costly fringe benefits such as pension plans.

Thus it's not surprising that some organizations demand an annual "housecleaning." As one chief executive officer told me:

"When the turnover is too low in our organization, I feel that managers are not doing their job. I expect them to dump deadwood. I want to make room for fresh talent. I don't want to nursemaid poor or mediocre performers."

NEGATIVE CONSEQUENCES OF TURNOVER

The most serious negative consequence of turnover is loss of valued employees. Sometimes, the losses are so great when key people depart that the organization suffers permanent harm. A classic example is the star salesman who carries customers from company to company. Or the research and development genius who transports a technological lead from one organization to another. And how many times have you seen smooth-running organizations become unglued because their leaders leave?

In the wake of turnover, disruption is common. Projects lose continuity. Key activities are interrupted. Mistakes flourish as overloaded employees try to fill in until replacements are hired and trained.

Another problem with turnover is that it may be epidemic. When employees leave an organization voluntarily, they often justify their departure by finding fault with their jobs. They may share their complaints with the employees who are staying and cause them to question their own satisfaction. Of course, an employee who leaves involuntarily will also complain to colleagues, influencing how they feel about their own jobs. Eventually the grapevine is ringing with sad stories about injustices and inequities. Thus a single termination may be accompanied by a series of terminations in rapid succession.

After reading about the pros and cons of turnover and the complexities of reporting turnover statistics, you may well be saying to yourself, "I can see why top management should be concerned about turnover and pay close attention to it, but I have a much more limited responsibility. How does all of this apply to me?"

Here are some commonsense guidelines for *all* managers with supervisory responsibility, even managers who have only a few people reporting to them.

COMMONSENSE ACTIONS

1. Keep your own turnover records. I recommend using a simple form like the one shown in Figure 4. Print each employee's name, job title, and hiring date on top of a 3" × 5" card. In the righthand corner, keep an ongoing record of the number of years the employee remains with the company and in the job. You need not make any other entries until the employee leaves. At that time, indicate the date of termination and the reasons for leaving. Indicate whether the termination was controllable or uncontrollable, whether it was voluntary or involuntary, and whether you had advance warning. Subsequently, keep track of how long the position is vacant and the amount of time and money it takes to recruit and train a qualified replacement.

2. Periodically review your records, trying to better understand turnover problems in your own unit rather than trying to explain away any situation that reflects badly on you.

Figure 4. Manager's personal turnover record.

Name _____ Years in

Title _____ company _____

Age _____ Sex _____ Job _____

1. *Hiring date*

2. *Termination date*

3. *Reasons for leaving* (controllable/uncontrollable; voluntary/involuntary)

4. *Costs of turnover* (vacancy period; recruitment/selection processing costs; training costs)

3. Look for trends over time. Perhaps you are supervising your people too closely or failing to provide enough training. Is there something you are doing, or *not* doing, that contributes to turnover?

4. When faced with turnover, ask yourself:

- Did I contribute in any way to an employee's decision to leave the organization?

- Am I considering terminating a valued employee for personal rather than sound business reasons?

- Have I avoided my responsibility as a manager by allowing poor performers to stay with the organization?

CHAPTER 2

Forced Versus Voluntary Termination

FORCED termination has a false air of respectability. Many managers I have worked with discount forced termination, claiming:

> "Our turnover statistics may be high, but we didn't want to keep many of the people who left anyway. We don't let deadwood accumulate in this company."

However, when I investigate the problem and find out more about the people "we didn't want to keep," I often find among the discards employees with strong capabilities who go on to build successful careers in other organizations.

There are good reasons why managers are reluctant to admit that they have forced capable people out of the organization. Obviously, one of the main reasons is that it "just doesn't look good" to let good people go or, worse yet, to force them to leave. So managers rationalize their decision to dismiss somebody, and in justifying it to others end up deceiving themselves.

Often, dismissal is a coverup for a manager's inability to cope with an uncooperative, troublemaking employee. Perhaps this tale of woe sounds familiar to you:

> "Mike was one of the most talented engineers I have ever supervised. But he was also the worst pain in my butt. He questioned everything I did. He always wanted to do things his way, resisting traditional policies and procedures. I would give in to him because I got tired of arguing with him. After a while, I couldn't tell whether I was supervising him or he was supervising me. Somebody had to go — either him or me."

One common reason managers hide the facts about a forced termination under the rug is that their decision may have been arbitrary. Afterward, when the emotions that led to the decision subside, they find it embarrassing to recall the circumstances that led to the dismissal.

FORCED TERMINATION

Many managers consider forced termination to be more respectable than voluntary termination. Indeed, in some organizations regular purges are the rule. Purging makes managers feel that they are ridding themselves of their problems. Usually, though, the causes of the problems remain, continuing to bring the same unfortunate results.

Typically, the employees who are purged are those who are "different" from the rest of the workforce. But the only difference may be that their work style is not the same as their managers'. Many managers like to hire in their own

image and want their subordinates to be "carbon copies."
This attitude can have serious consequences. For example:

> The director of a research and development department
> was a loner. He interacted with his subordinates mini-
> mally, usually only to transmit instructions. Following
> his example, his subordinates "minded their own busi-
> ness." This work style led to lack of coordination and
> uncooperativeness that seriously reduced the productiv-
> ity of the laboratory.

In the face of economic downturns, even organizations
that don't advocate purging may view forced termination
as a way of achieving highly visible cost savings. Managers win official pats on the head from top management
when they demonstrate a concern for improving profit. So
they reduce the workforce, particularly the higher-priced
staff members: the termination of one $30,000-a-year em-
ployee is equivalent to the termination of two $15,000-a-
year employees.

Whether purging is done in the name of upgrading the
workforce or improving profits, human resources are
wasted in the process. Often, an organization has invested
heavily in the training and development of employees
who represent a unique and valuable repository of experience. So the short-term benefits gained from terminating
these employees are more than offset by the long-term
effects of their loss.

VOLUNTARY TERMINATION

Often, work conditions within the organization contribute to an employee's decision to leave. An employee may
be only one step ahead of a dismissal. He knows his days
are numbered and chooses to avoid the embarrassment of
dismissal. He may be failing because he can't perform the
job or can't meet what he feels are the unrealistic expectations of his supervisor.

Sometimes, a job or organization has been "wrong" for an employee from the very start—or changing conditions turn a "right" job into a "wrong" job. In either case, the employee escapes by leaving the organization.

Occasionally, employees are pushed out of an organization by the deliberate actions of their supervisors. For example, an employee is passed up for promotion. She receives minimal or no merit increases. She is given an overload of "scut" work. And her manager continually searches for mistakes, confronting her regularly with, "I got yuh!" Because many organizations require an official explanation and documentation when an employee is dismissed, the "set up" is common: it enables the manager to get rid of an employee with no questions asked.

Sometimes, a voluntary resignation is a cover up for an injustice, as it was in the following case:

The general manager of a branch office of a large office equipment manufacturer resigned unexpectedly. The branch office had been a model of efficiency and productivity, and the general manager was highly regarded by top management. Since he left with no immediate job prospect in sight and gave only a vague explanation, I was asked as an independent consultant to talk to him.

The manager claimed to be completely satisfied with his job and the organization and discussed his many positive experiences. When I asked him about his reasons for leaving, he mentioned the "need to try something else" and the desire for faster growth than the organization could provide.

Eventually, by persistent questioning, I was able to get him to reveal the events that led up to his voluntary resignation. About a year before his departure, his immediate supervisor received a below-average performance appraisal. Most of the branch offices under the supervisor's control were performing poorly, with the notable exception of the office of the manager I was interviewing. Thereafter the situation worsened, and top management kept claiming that if all the other branches were as well managed as this "model" branch, the supervisor would not be in trouble. The supervisor became increasingly intimidated and began to feel that the top-performing branch manager was being groomed sub rosa as his replacement. So he set out to force the branch manager to resign in order to remove his competition.

Except in extraordinary situations like the one just described, voluntary termination is often regarded as "no fault" turnover. A pervasive attitude is, "It couldn't be helped." Besides, when unusual cases of voluntary turnover are investigated, it often comes down to one person's word against another's. And in these situations the *manager's code* dictates: "When in doubt, the manager is always right."

Of course, voluntary turnover may be legitimately "no fault." The decision to leave may be a natural consequence of the conflict between individual needs and goals and organizational needs and goals.

For example, a talented, high performer may feel that a slow-growing organization with low management turnover offers a limited opportunity for advancement. By changing jobs, he can accelerate his career. Or an employee may resign voluntarily to continue her education. An employee may decide to move to another part of the country, perhaps because another member of the family has been transferred. Sometimes an employee will change jobs because he has grown tired of his present career. Or an employee may decide that she doesn't like a particular industry or is attracted to another industry.

It makes good sense to carefully assess the legitimacy of both voluntary and involuntary turnover, trying to determine to what extent it represents "no fault." This is not to suggest an organizational witchhunt, seeking out a scapegoat for every turnover statistic. But it does mean that an organization should make sure it is not wasting human resources by arbitrarily or unjustly terminating employees or forcing them to leave voluntarily.

COMMONSENSE ACTIONS

1. *Separation interview.* Managers can use the simple form shown in Figure 5 to make an accurate assessment of resignations and dismissals. The departing employee should be encouraged to answer the six questions on the form fully and candidly.

○ *What are the best parts of your job?* If the employee doesn't respond with sufficient information, probe further, asking about specific duties, relationships, working conditions, and so on.

○ *What are the worst parts of your job?* The employee will probably resist this question, particularly if the conditions under which he is leaving are strained. In that case, try to convince the employee that you will *accept* what-

Figure 5. Separation interview.

1. What are the best parts of your job? Why?

2. What are the worst parts of your job? Why?

3. What aspects of your manager's style do you like best?

4. What aspects of your manager's style do you like least?

5. What recommendations would you make for improvements?

6. What, if anything, could have prolonged your employment?

ever he says as being worthy of careful consideration. In a sense, you should welcome "negative" information without becoming defensive, because it can help you in making improvements.

o *What aspects of your manager's style do you like the best?* When you ask this question, explain that you are not fishing for compliments, but want to know what things you are doing well and should continue to do in the future.

o *What aspects of your manager's style do you like the least?* Many employees, not wishing to "burn their bridges behind them," may not want to answer this question. If that happens, you might try an approach like this:

EMPLOYEE   I didn't really dislike anything in particular about your style.

MANAGER   I know I do a lot of things wrong. And I'm concerned that I may continue to do them wrong in the future—and hurt my subordinates in the process. I need constructive criticism.

EMPLOYEE   *(Still resisting)* I just can't think of anything.

MANAGER   Perhaps it would help if we reviewed specific areas, such as how closely I supervised you and how fairly I appraised you.

EMPLOYEE   *(Cautiously, watching for reaction from the manager)* Well, I wasn't completely happy about my last appraisal.

MANAGER   Tell me about it.

Gradually, the employee should open up as the manager prompts him to reveal the sources of his dissatisfaction.

o *What recommendations would you make for improvements?* Even though the employee will not benefit personally from improvements, his comments can be of help to colleagues. An appeal to the future welfare of associates will usually elicit a response. The employee may suggest sweeping changes which can't be acted upon. In this case, try to elicit more specific and practical suggestions.

o *What, if anything, could have prolonged your employment?* This is one of the most important questions that you will ask the departing employee. His answers will give you insights into the extent to which his resignation was controllable. Often, even when the employee is leaving primarily for personal reasons, he will have a number of complaints. Such information, though exaggerated, can provide useful leads for making improvements.

2. *Documentation of termination.* Whenever an employee is terminated involuntarily, you should prepare a *documentation of termination* for the record. (See Figure 6.) This form serves a double purpose: it makes the reason for the termination (1) part of the official record and (2) clear to the employee. Too often, a terminated employee will say, "I don't know why I was fired."

In preparing the form, keep in mind that you will be called upon to defend the entries, either by the departing employee or, subsequently, by an official inquiry. Therefore, support the entries with as much evidence as you can gather. Discuss only observable, measurable performance

Figure 6. Documentation of termination.

Name _____ Date _____

Title _____ Department _____

---

1. *Performance deficiencies*

2. *Unacceptable behavior*

_____   _____
Manager   *Employee*

deficiencies, unacceptable behavior, and significant undesirable events. Above all, don't try to play amateur psychologist, talking about poor attitudes or motivation. As soon as you start discussing *why* somebody does something, you are on weak ground.

It is important to prepare the form *before* you officially decide to terminate someone, because in the process of gathering evidence you may realize that you don't have a defendable case. Impersonal fact-gathering often neutralizes some of the emotional content of a termination decision.

As a final commonsense action, post a sign in a prominent position in your office that reads, "When an employee leaves, don't assume *no fault!*"

CHAPTER 3

The Stayers

WHEN people don't like something, they naturally want to get away from it. Often, when leaving a job is not a viable alternative, employees will stay—and withdraw. They may reduce the amount of time they spend on the job by increased absences and lateness. And they may suffer silently, insulating themselves from their jobs by turning off.

Because withdrawal on the job is not highly visible, it deserves careful attention. In many ways, the reasons dissatisfied employees stay on the job are just as important as the reasons they leave. Consider the case of two dissatisfied employees in identical jobs. Both are market analysts, working under an intolerable manager. He is overcontrolling, overdemanding, insensitive, and disrespectful, and he provides minimal leadership.

One of the analysts has a strong self-image and is very independent and mobile. After just one year in the job assignment, he finds another opportunity in a large company in another state—and becomes a turnover statistic.

The other analyst has a poor self-image; she is dependent and immobile. She feels that there are no alternatives open to her, particularly since her husband likes his job and is reluctant to relocate. She began as a secretary in the department and considers herself lucky to have been promoted to higher responsibility. Even though she has been in the job four years, has mastered many new skills, and has performed exceptionally, she feels that other companies may not want, as she describes herself, "an ex-secretary and amateur market research analyst." Thus she stays—and becomes a turn-off casualty.

Companies may attract immobile employees, or create conditions that foster immobility. Such companies will probably experience very low turnover and may be unaware of a serious developing problem of withdrawal-while-staying. For example:

A division of a large heavy-equipment company has a sales force with a median age of 45. Most of the sales representatives have been with the company for 10 years or more. The turnover rate for this very secure, high-paying job is less than 2 percent annually. Most of the customers are long-term clients who are loyal to the company's unique, well-respected products. The sales representatives do not have to sell the products aggressively. All they have to do to protect the business is service the customers regularly.

Competitors are far overshadowed by this company. Thus their products are harder to sell and their pay scales are much lower. It's unlikely that they could pirate away any of the company's sales representatives.

So, the company's representatives stay in an undemanding, high-paying job that becomes routine and unchallenging. Their salaries increase steadily from year to year, while their interest and productivity decline.

Although the low turnover and poor morale described in this case are exceptional, the job immobility is not. Many employees will stay in a job until something happens to "push" or "pull" them from the organization. In fact, most organizations have a number of dissatisfied employees who should not stay with the company. They remain not because they want to, but because they believe they have to stay.

Employees who stay because they want to are more likely to give their full commitment to the organization than the reluctant stayers. Usually, they are satisfied with the job content and work environment. Thus it makes a significant difference whether employees are staying for "right" or "wrong" reasons.

Employees who stay for the "right" reasons usually describe the job as "going well." What this means is that there is a good match between their experience and their expectations. They expect work assignments to be challenging and anticipate making full use of their skills. They expect reasonable supervision, training, and development. They expect an opportunity for growth. They anticipate fair pay and benefits, good working conditions, and compatible working companions. They expect to perform well and to have their performance recognized by others. They expect to work for an organization they can be proud of. They expect to have a job that will give them reasonable free time and that will not impinge on their personal lives.

While all these expectations may not be explicitly stated or even fully recognized by employees when they accept the job, they exist nevertheless. And if employees perceive that their expectations are not being met, they will consider leaving the organization.

However, employees will tolerate some dissonance and

may not perceive that things are not "going well" unless there are extreme or highly visible shortfalls in expectations. When that happens, employees will pay closer attention to the matching of expectations and experience, and even minor differences will be magnified in importance.

Employees who stay for the "wrong" reasons sense that things are not going well but feel that there are more compelling reasons to stay than to leave. The "wrong" reasons to stay can be classified into four categories: personal reasons, family reasons, work environment reasons, and timing reasons. Let's take a closer look at each of these four categories.

PERSONAL REASONS

At the top of the list of personal reasons are poor self-image and lack of self-confidence. Even top performers may feel insecure about themselves. They attribute their present high achievement to being in the "right place at the right time" or to just plain luck. They question their ability to do well in a higher-level job or in another organization. However, those around them—supervisors, peers, family members—continually prod them to seek advancement and label them as "lacking in ambition."

Low expectations are another common reason for overstaying in a job and in an organization. With an air of resignation, employees accept less than satisfactory working conditions. They don't like what's happening, but they fail to do anything about it because they don't expect more. For example:

John Evans is a talented engineer. He comes from a working-class background and is the first one in his family to have completed a college education and to work as a professional. He has been in the same job for five years, and for three of those years he hasn't broadened his responsibilities or developed any new skills. Less-talented peers have left the organization for better-paying, more responsible jobs. John stays, continually losing interest in his job and slipping in performance, because he never expected to be more than "just an engineer."

Unlike John Evans, some people have high expectations which they feel they cannot realize because of *visible* differences. Certainly, some women and minorities justly feel there are roadblocks ahead of them. Older employees also feel stymied. Overweight people, unattractive people, and people with speech impediments and a variety of other physical *differences* may encounter informal, unspoken opposition to their progress.

Other people have a clear road to advancement, but they act as if there were obstacles ahead. Perhaps they have difficulty making decisions. So they "wait and see" what will happen to them rather than trying to influence the direction of their careers. Or they take the first steps toward making a career change and then back away from an opportunity within easy reach. For example:

Susan Tyler stays in a job that she says she can "do with her eyes closed." On numerous occasions she was offered better opportunities within her own organization and in other organizations. Each time she had an opportunity, she gave a rational explanation for declining. But she knew that she was acting out of fear. As she described the feeling to intimates, "I just got cold feet. I was fearful of change, of stepping into an unknown situation."

FAMILY REASONS

An employee may be held back from leaving a job for family reasons. These can be just as binding as personal reasons. Generally, family reasons fall into two broad categories: community ties and family obligations.

A family becomes attached to a community in many ways. Certainly, a large number of relatives and friends in the community will anchor the family. Involvement in social groups and activities can also tie a family to a community. People hesitate to leave cherished homes in which they have invested money and attention. And they are naturally reluctant to leave familiar places in which they feel comfortable.

Even if employees are willing to sever community ties, they may have family obligations that prevent them from leaving. Perhaps they have elderly parents in town and feel obligated to care for them. Or they may be hesitant to disrupt the education of their children and thrust them into a new school environment. A spouse may be employed in a desirable job in the community and may be reluctant to leave. Whatever the reason, it acts as an anchor to keep the employee in an undesirable job.

WORK ENVIRONMENT REASONS

In addition to personal and family reasons for staying in the job, there are some "wrong" work-related reasons for staying. High on the list are seniority rights. Organizations attempt to lock in employees by awarding special benefits to stayers. Some organizations relate advancement and the accumulation of retirement benefits to seniority. The perquisites vary greatly but generally favor long-term employees.

Another work-related reason for staying is job specialization. What employees do for one company may not be suitable for another. Or the supply of people available may exceed the demand for a particular specialty. The lack of transferrable skills—skills that can be applied in other jobs—is a serious handicap for employees desiring a job change.

Although seniority and job specialization are legitimate and compelling reasons for staying in a job, they become the "wrong" reasons to stay when employees hate their jobs. Productivity and work quality suffer, and neither the corporation nor the employee is benefited.

There may be a lack of job alternatives for reasons other than specialization. Perhaps an industry is in a depressed condition. Possibly job requirements have been upgraded, and many employees seeking jobs will need retraining in order to qualify. Often job alternatives exist, but employees are not aware of them. Sometimes employees don't realize that they could qualify for job openings because they view their skills narrowly.

Employees may find job opportunities lacking because they have a nonmarketable work record. Possibly, they've been in the same job too long, and potential employers feel that they lack ambition or have some other shortcoming. Their present employer may have a bad reputation. Or their own reputation may have been damaged by poor appraisal ratings or some other "black mark" on their record.

TIMING REASONS

The final category of "wrong" reasons for staying in a job relates to timing. When an opportunity presents itself, the employee feels it's just not the "right time" to make a job change. Perhaps the family is recovering from some crisis and the employee feels family members are emotionally unable to cope with a change. Or the employee may have been divorced and may be unwilling to move too far away from his children until they become accustomed to the change in the family. Or an employee may have moved several times in the last few years and may feel that she must wait a while before making another move. Perhaps the employee expects positive changes in the organization and is waiting to see what will happen.

There are numerous reasons to delay changing jobs. But whenever the delay extends beyond the point where a job change would be logical and desirable, the employee will become increasingly dissatisfied. Thus low turnover can hurt an organization rather than help it. And the people who stay may be unhappy, uncommitted, and unproductive.

COMMONSENSE ACTIONS

1. Pay close attention to why people stay in a job and with the organization. Questioning them about why they are staying should become a routine part of every appraisal interview. Some of the questions you might ask are:
- Would you have any objections to a job change at this time?
- Do you feel you are ready for a job change?
- What are your main reasons for staying in your current job?

These questions are designed to reveal the employee's attitudes about change and to uncover anything that might make the employee a reluctant stayer.

2. For each employee under your supervision, develop a *vulnerability index.* (See Figure 7.) Rate the positive work-related events that have happened to the employee in the past year—for example, merit increases, added job variety, and added responsibility. Use a 1 ("slightly positive") to 5 ("very positive") scale. Then rate the negative events that contributed to the employee's dissatisfaction—for example, failure to be promoted, poor performance rating, and interpersonal problems with peers or supervisors. Use a 1 ("slightly negative") to 5 ("very negative") scale.

3. Total the ratings of the positive and negative events. Then divide the positive total by the negative total and multiply the answer by 100. The higher the index number, the less vulnerable the employee. For example, an employee may have had four very positive events in the past year and four slightly negative events. The total of the positives is 20; the total of the negatives is 4. Thus the vulnerability index is 20/4 = 5 × 100 = 500. On the other

Figure 7. Vulnerability index.

Date: Year ending December 19 __

1. Positive events	Rating				
	Low				High
Merit increase	1	2	3	④	5
Added variety	1	2	③	4	5
Added responsibility	1	2	3	④	5
Special recognition	1	2	③	4	5
Total					14

2. Negative events	Rating				
	Low				High
Passed over for promotion	1	2	3	4	⑤
Poor performance rating	1	2	3	4	⑤
Interpersonal problems	1	2	③	4	5
Total					13

3. Calculation of index $\dfrac{14}{13} = 1.08 \times 100 = 108$

hand, the employee may have had four very negative events and four slightly positive events. The total of the positives is 4; the total of the negatives is 20. The vulnerability index is 4/20 = .20 × 100 = 20.

4. Managers are well advised to determine the *positive* reasons employees stay in a job and with an organization. By talking with employees about their sources of satisfaction, managers can better assess what they can do to make the work environment motivating to a larger number of employees.

The manager might initiate a dialogue as follows:

MANAGER   Ann, I'm impressed with the enthusiasm you have for your job, and your loyalty to me and the company. Obviously, not all the employees in this organization feel the same way. What do you feel accounts for the difference in attitude?

EMPLOYEE   I don't know. I never really thought about it. I know what makes me happy, but I'm not sure about the others.

MANAGER   I don't expect you to speak for the others. Just tell me about yourself and why you derive satisfaction from the job and the company.

Discussions like this, with committed and productive employees, reveal valuable insights into why employees want to stay in their jobs. Instead of getting this information from impersonal survey results, the manager can hear it directly from his or her employees.

CHAPTER 4

The Leavers

WHILE everybody in an organization is a potential leaver, depending on conditions, certain classes of employees are much more likely to leave than others. The more you know about them, the more you are in a position to intervene and, hopefully, to save worthwhile employees.

One way of better understanding the leavers is to take a two-dimensional look at them, using the graph shown in Figure 8. One dimension of the graph is the career stage of the employee; the other dimension is the extent to which the employee is being pushed or pulled from the job and/or organization.

The propensity to leave changes at different career stages. Certainly, an employee is more likely to leave in

Figure 8. Two-dimensional view of leavers.

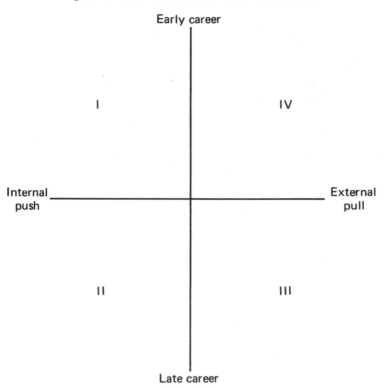

early career stages than in later career stages. The extent to which the employee finds the internal work environment hostile and/or the external work environment attractive also influences the propensity to leave. This dimension is often related to career stage as well.

To better understand how to use the graph, let's examine four case histories, representing points within each of the quadrants.

Shirley Katz is 27 and has a master's degree in political science. When she completed graduate school, she was unable to find employment related to her education. Instead, she accepted a position as a sales representative for a large pharmaceuticals company. She has performed well in that position and feels that she deserves advancement. But the logical next career step is district manager, and there are no female district managers in her company—and few of them in the industry. However, she feels she can become the first female district manager, or perhaps get promoted to the marketing staff. She belongs in quadrant I.

Dave Robins just received his 20-year service pin from a small printing company. He is the office manager and in that capacity wears many different hats. Recently, the family that owned the company sold its interests to a large organization and retired from the business. Now Dave is working with supervisors he doesn't like, under conditions he finds unbearable. He plans to leave even though he doesn't have any job prospects. If necessary, he will buy a small business. He belongs in quadrant II.

Tony Dominick has worked for three different companies in the last 15 years and has progressed rapidly. He is currently controller, responsible for a highly profitable division of a major business machines company. He is well known in his industry and other industries because he is an officer of the Accounting Association and publishes frequently in their journal. As a result, executive search firms approach him regularly with job offers. He feels the time is ripe to move into general management and is planning to accept an attractive offer. He belongs in quadrant III.

Dave Middleton is 25. Since leaving graduate school, he has worked in two different organizations. Because of his outstanding scholastic record and his demonstrated ability to assume responsibility quickly, his talents are highly marketable, and he knows it. At this early stage of his career he wants to climb as high as he can and feels he can do that best by changing organizations. He belongs in quadrant IV.

Whether employees feel a "push" or "pull" to leave may be related to their own expectations, and not necessarily to the work environment. Some employees think of themselves as riding a "fast track." They want to move upward as fast as they can. If the company can't clear the track for them, they will move elsewhere. Both they and their families will make whatever sacrifices are necessary to further their careers.

Usually, the fast-trackers are high performers whose abilities are acknowledged by others. They are accustomed to getting special attention and rewards. Their positive self-image is reinforced regularly by their supervisors and by others around them. They expect growth—in rewards, in responsibilities, and in opportunities for developing their skills.

Other employees perceive themselves as being on a more traditional "slow track." They are willing to accept delays and setbacks in their careers. They often adopt a wait-and-see attitude, hoping that loyalty will be rewarded and that the company will take care of them. They tolerate slow growth, or no growth. They make minimum demands on the organization, because they don't expect any "special" rewards.

The propensity to leave an organization is also influenced by an employee's perception of available opportunities. Some employees believe, perhaps without any justification, that their skills are highly marketable and job opportunities are readily available. Their optimism may be based on a demonstrated proficiency in their jobs or on the fact that they have developed highly specialized and desirable skills. They may have accumulated "good contacts" in other companies. Perhaps, their industry is expanding or there is a shortage of qualified people in the section of the country in which they live. Usually, they are confident about their ability to sell their talent to potential employers: they know how to look for a job, and how to put their best foot forward.

Equally talented employees may be much more pessimistic about job opportunities. They may not recognize that they have transferrable skills and may think of themselves as qualifying for only specific job titles. They underestimate themselves and their ability to find another job. They may feel they are anchored to a particular industry or area of the country, not realizing that "the pickings are better elsewhere."

An employee's value system can also influence his or her desire to leave the organization. In a sense, leavers can be described as employees whose value systems are mismatched with the work environment. Figure 9 is an adaptation of a classification system developed by Dr. John I. Holland, who described six different kinds of value systems: conventional, realistic, social, investigative, enterprising, and artistic.

The employee with a *conventional* value system feels most comfortable in an orderly work environment. He enjoys structure, knowing exactly what's expected of him.

Figure 9. Value system classifications.

Value System	Friendly Work Environment	Hostile Work Environment
Conventional	Ordered	Freewheeling
Realistic	Traditional	Nontraditional
Social	Warm	Cold
Investigative	Challenging	Routine
Enterprising	Materialistic	Egalitarian
Artistic	Creative	Rule-bound

This chart is based on classifications developed by John I. Holland, *Making Vocational Choices; A Theory of Careers*, Englewood Cliffs, N.J., Prentice-Hall, 1973.

He operates in a no-nonsense, unimaginative way. He would be unhappy in a freewheeling, unstructured work environment in which people operated in an emotional, unconventional, and unpredictable way.

Employees with a *realistic* value system are also comfortable in an orderly rather than freewheeling work environment. They prefer to work on simple, tangible, and traditional activities. The work environment becomes hostile for them when they are asked to take on uncharted, nontraditional assignments in which they must decide how to perform a task. They prefer to "go by the book" rather than rely on their own initiative.

For employees with a *social* value system, the accomplishment of a task is secondary to the maintenance of social relationships. They thrive in a work environment in which people are friendly, understanding, and cooperative. They are unhappy in a work environment in which there is conflict and dog-eat-dog competitiveness.

The employee with *investigative* values is primarily task-oriented. She thrives in an environment that provides a steady flow of intellectually challenging assignments. The environment becomes hostile for her when she is forced to spend her time in routine activities and when others deal with her on an emotional rather than rational basis.

The employee with *enterprising* values is interested in the return for his efforts: money, power, and status. He's ambitious and materialistic. He is happy in an environment in which his contribution is highly visible and there is a direct relationship between contribution and rewards. The environment becomes hostile for him when he has to suppress his self-interests and operate as an invisible member of the team. He is far too ambitious and acquisitive to accept an equal share of money, power, and status.

Employees with an *artistic* value system have a strong need to express their originality and individuality. They are happiest in an unconventional, flexible work environment in which creativity is valued. They are unhappy in a rule-bound work environment that forces them to conform. They would be highly dissatisfied in the traditional work environment valued by people with conventional and realistic value systems.

In addition to value differences, one or more critical incidents may contribute to an employee's decision to leave. Perhaps an employee is forced to accept a new work assignment which she considers undesirable or which forces her to relocate in an area of the country in which she doesn't want to live. Possibly, she feels she is the victim of inequity: in salary progression, work assignment, promotion, or distribution of workload. An organizational change may suddenly make the work environment hostile. Perhaps an unfriendly management has assumed command or a profit improvement program threatens the employee's security. Often, these critical incidents are blown out of proportion by the employee's fears and vivid imagination.

One type of leaver who appears to be especially intolerant of "things not going right" is the *job hopper.* He is perpetually searching for the right niche. He is a highly ambitious and energetic person desperately trying to accelerate his climb upward. Often, he is not sure about what's "right" for him but is quick to see what's "wrong." For example, I interviewed a young man who had had four different jobs in seven years. He reported:

> "I'm not sure about what I want specifically, except I want to make a lot of money and hold an important job. When I first take a job, it's not with the intention that I'm going to move on after one or two years. But invariably I become disenchanted, feeling my forward movement is blocked, I'm not learning, or I have not made friends in high places. So I look for more favorable conditions."

Unfortunately, after a few job moves the job hopper develops a reputation for being an opportunist without loyalty to the company. And loyalty is considered to be an important attribute in many organizations.

Job hoppers aren't the only ones who get accused of disloyalty. In many organizations, any voluntary termination is considered an act of disloyalty. Thus all leavers are labeled disloyal employees. But leavers are not less loyal than stayers; they are just less willing to tolerate unacceptable conditions. Whether they feel their talents are being misused, their rate of growth is inadequate, or a recent change in the work environment is intolerable, they refuse to sit back and hope for things to improve. Instead, they assume the risk of searching for a new work environment in which conditions will be better.

The difference between a leaver and a stayer was described to me by a chemical engineer:

"Everybody in my department was miserable. We were underpaid; we worked for a tyrant. The work wasn't challenging: it could have been performed by technicians with far less education and experience. The only difference between me and them was that I was willing to do something about it. I knew that I might be going from the frying pan into the fire, because it's hard to find out in advance exactly what a new job and a new company will be like. But I believed the potential gain was worth the risk."

COMMONSENSE ACTIONS

1. Take a two-dimensional view of each of your subordinates and position them on the graph in Figure 8. Subordinates in quadrants I and II are likely to be "stayers"; those in quadrants III and IV are likely to be "leavers." Try to determine if employees are likely to stay or leave for "right" or "wrong" reasons.

2. Assess the value systems of your subordinates. Then analyze the work environment and decide if it's friendly or hostile to them. Next, develop a list of ways in which

you can make the work environment more friendly for all your subordinates. For example, you might give more freedom of action to employees with an "enterprising" or "artistic" value system.

3. The best way to deal with the job hopper is look for that work pattern in candidates for employment. Unless you can offer the job hopper an opportunity for advancement after a short length of time, don't hire him.

4. Consider organizing periodic roundtable discussions with members of your staff. During these discussions, solicit their feelings about why employees have left the organization in the past or are considering leaving it now. You should not be an active participant in the discussions. Instead, get your staff members to think about the problem and to contribute their ideas.

The roundtable discussions will give employees an opportunity to air their concerns indirectly. It is common for people to project their own feelings onto others. Thus when a staff member says, "I know that some of the people who left were upset about the lack of variety in their jobs," he may be talking about his own feelings.

Most important, many of your staff members may have been privy to confidential information from colleagues who have left. Their comments can provide insights that you would not normally have gotten.

5. Managers have a tendency to treat younger and older employees the same, assuming that the needs of each group are identical. However, both the age of an employee and his or her length of service influence the employee's needs. For example, an employee in his fifties who has been in a job for 15 years may have reconciled himself to the fact that his career is stalled and may be primarily concerned about job security. In contrast, an employee in her twenties who has been in the same job for less than three years may be primarily concerned about advancement.

Thus, in making decisions about career development, al-

ways take the needs of employees into account. Ask yourself:

- How will older or younger employees be affected by
  the action I'm about to take?
- Will long-term employees be affected differently by
  my action than short-term employees?
- How will other groups (women, minorities, and so on)
  be affected by my action?

CHAPTER 5

Turn-Off

WHEN employees stay with an organization for the wrong reasons—personal, family, work environment, or timing—a special kind of turnover occurs. The employees leave psychologically. They are on the job physically but not mentally.

This psychological turnover, or turn-off, can have serious consequences, particularly because it can go undetected for years. Perhaps you recognize these typical turned-off employees:

Pete M. is a troublemaker. He's been with the company for 15 years and has held his current job for 7. He claims he doesn't like being taken advantage of and refuses to do anything *extra*, anything over and above what is officially expected of him. Whenever the workload spirals or something out of the ordinary is requested, he is the first to complain and usually succeeds in influencing others.

Ellen R. is a long-term employee who has been in her current job for over five years. She is concerned about her stalled career, but she suppresses her anger. She feels "it's not fair" that she has been forgotten and neglected. However, rather than becoming belligerent about the "injustice" done to her, she has isolated herself from the rest of the organization. She goes about her daily chores, interacting minimally with others and doing what she must do to get by. She has few friends at work, and certainly doesn't enjoy her job.

Allen W. is another uncommitted employee. He looks for any escape from the drudgery of his present work assignment. Although he has been in the job for only three years, he wants "out." He feels that the only way to step up to a better job is to get special training. So, at the expense of the company, he has gone back to school, studying for an MBA in a field that is unrelated to his current responsibilities. According to Allen, his degree will be his ticket to a better future. Meanwhile, he stays on and only tolerates his current job.

Larry G. is very content. He has a job that he performs easily, within a 9-to-5 day. In fact, he finds time to carry on nonbusiness-related activities during the day, spending at least an hour a day writing letters and talking on the phone to meet his responsibilities as a school board member in the local community. As he describes it, "Work supplies the food for the table, but the *kicks* come from the school board activities." Larry doesn't care if he ever gets promoted and prefers a nondemanding job.

THE EFFECTS OF TURN-OFF

Turn-off has many serious consequences. Some of the most common and most troublesome are described below.

Work Performance

Turn-off is directly related to a reduction in the quantity and quality of performance. Whether an employee holds back anger, withdraws psychologically, or shifts primary interest from work to outside activities, the result is the same—decreased productivity.

In every workforce, many of the average-to-low performers are victims of turn-off. As their commitment to the job goes, so goes their energy and initiative. They walk through the motions, rarely applying themselves fully to their work assignments.

Attitudes and Behavior

Turned-off employees have self-defeating attitudes. They're frustrated, disappointed, hostile, vindictive, envious, and worried. These attitudes affect them on and off the job. They compromise both their physical and mental health. While the organization and the job may be the focus of their unhappiness, it carries over to their personal lives and affects their relationships with family and friends. It interferes with their ability to enjoy life.

Turned-off employees are bored, indifferent, and uncommitted. Sometimes, they are argumentative and uncooperative. In either case, they are not pleasant to be with. Thus they alienate others, just at the time when they need support the most. Typically, they sound like this:

"When my old boss left, the job never felt the same. He was my best booster. My new boss frequently found fault with my work. After a while, I said, 'What's the use?' I didn't try as hard and, frankly, I didn't do that good a job. I didn't relate well to the eager beavers, and I found myself identifying with one man in the department who shared my dissatisfaction. Eventually, we isolated ourselves from the rest of the group. And when he was terminated, I felt all alone."

Effects on Others
Malcontented turn-offs can have a profound effect on others. Their low productivity can place an extra workload on co-workers. Their uncooperativeness can create bottlenecks and contribute to missed deadlines. Their unhappiness can lower the morale of the work group, and their hostility and vindictiveness can lead to widespread conflict.

Lack of Growth
Often turned-off employees lose interest in personal growth. They feel that there will be no return on any investment in self-development. The longer they remain in the same job, the less they feel the need to strengthen their skills. Typically, they express their feelings about growth as follows:

"After five years in this job, I know how to do my work Nobody's going to tell me something that will make a big difference in how well I perform. Besides, why should I waste my time in self-development activities that won't lead to a promotion, or even to a raise?"

Loss of Commitment
Generally, employees who feel frustrated and disappointed are not committed to the job, the boss, or the company. Loyalty and commitment usually depend on a feeling of reciprocity: "I'll give it if I get it." Thus, when things are going reasonably well, turned-off employees will get the job done with minimal effort. But when special demands are made of them, they won't put forth the extra time and effort necessary to get the job done.

Their lack of commitment can have serious consequences. When the company encounters a serious problem they just give up, allowing the problem to get out of control and cause irreparable damage. Or, when the workload gets too heavy, they complain, drag their heels, and miss deadlines. They become more of a hindrance than a help.

COMMONSENSE ACTIONS

As a manager you cannot ignore the adverse consequences of "employee turn-off." They won't get better, and they won't go away. Nor can you afford to tell the numerous turned-off employees in your organization to "shape up or ship out." Replacement with qualified employees may be a costly, time-consuming process. And after just a few short years, the new employees may become turned off. Instead of ignoring them, here are some commonsense actions you can take.

1. Calmly schedule a meeting with each turned-off employee and share your feelings. For example:

MANAGER   I'm concerned because I feel that you're not as satisfied in your job as you have been in the past.

SUBORDINATE   What do you mean? The job's okay.

MANAGER   Well, you've been in the same job for five years. Your performance ratings have been lower in the last two years than they were in previous years. (*The manager describes the relevant facts.*)

SUBORDINATE   Can you blame me for letting down a little on the job? I really worked hard for several years, and what did it get me?

MANAGER   I appreciate how you feel, but is turning off on the job helping you? (*The manager tries to get the subordinate to understand that his attitudes and behavior are self-defeating.*)

2. Even though employees have let down on the job, you can't afford to let them continue to do so in the future. You should set high standards and negotiate specific improvement objectives. For example:

MANAGER   Now that we've established the serious consequences of turning off on the job, let's discuss reasonable expectations for your performance in the future.

EMPLOYEE Okay, I'll work harder.

MANAGER I appreciate your willingness to work harder. But let's define the areas in which you intend to invest extra time and effort and the results we can expect. (*The manager negotiates with the employee for a commitment to specific improvement objectives.*)

3. Managers tend to "ride" employees who are turned-off. Supposedly, the employees will respond to managerial urgings, such as:

"You can do better."

"Get the job done or else."

"Somebody who has been around as long as you should know better."

Not only do these appeals normally fall on deaf ears, but they may further turn off employees. Instead, the turned-off employee needs the support of the manager and reinforcement of any action that demonstrates a change in the right direction. For example:

MANAGER That's a very insightful report you submitted. It's obvious you really know the subject.

OR

MANAGER Thank you for working late last night. I really appreciated your help. Now, how would you like to take on that special project you wanted?

By the way the manager behaves, he or she demonstrates that the job can be less frustrating and less disappointing if the employee performs in a way that merits immediate rewards.

4. Managers don't help turned-off employees by ignoring slipping performance and negative attitudes. Often, these are indicators that the employees need attention. A manager can respond to this need by making it a habit of initiating casual discussions with employees and involving them in group activities:

MANAGER Hi, Charlie. How's it going?

EMPLOYEE Nothing special happening.

MANAGER I noticed you didn't have much to say at the last staff meeting. In the past I've heard you express many ideas on the topic we were discussing.

EMPLOYEE I guess I was just feeling out of it.

MANAGER The topic is going to be on the agenda again next meeting. Why don't you prepare a short presentation? I'd like to have some of the other people hear your ideas.

5. A very effective way of regaining the interest of turned-off employees is to stimulate their desire for personal growth and learning. This doesn't mean sending the employees "to a course or two" or relying on others to assume the burden for their training and development. Rather, it means taking the initiative yourself:

MANAGER Did you see this article in the current issue of *Business Week?*

EMPLOYEE No, I didn't.

MANAGER Why don't you read it? There are some ideas in it I'd like to discuss with you.

OR

MANAGER I've called in a consultant to help us with the project. I'd like you to work closely with him and "pick his brains" so that next time you can serve as an internal consultant.

To summarize the commonsense actions, always talk to turned-off employees. Establish a continuing dialogue with them. Don't accept turned-off performance and help turned-off employees regain interest in and commitment to the job.

CHAPTER 6

The Turnover Process

THE decision to terminate an employee, voluntarily or involuntarily, is the final and anticlimactic event in a process that starts when the employee is hired. From a psychological point of view, termination occurs long before it actually takes place.

However, the turnover process is invisible to onlookers, as evidenced by their surprised remarks:

"It was a shock when Beth left. She was a top performer and was well liked by her supervisors and peers. She had progressed well since she came to work for the company about five years ago. She rarely complained and appeared to like her job."

Yet Beth decided to leave three years ago. At that time, she confirmed a first impression she had received during her orientation into the company: there appeared to be a ceiling on the level a woman could reach. During her first few years of employment, she had watched many competent women become stalled in their careers. She resolved to stay long enough to build a marketable work record and skills, and then to go elsewhere for advancement.

In contrast to Beth's resignation, Sandy's departure came as no surprise. He left under very different circumstances. He was fired after a loud argument with his boss. According to the grapevine, Sandy and the boss "never got along." They were a classic oil-and-water team.

In reality, even though they fought frequently and loudly, they worked well together—too well. Sandy's boss was a dependent person who wanted a strong man like Sandy to rely on. And Sandy, who was independent and strong-minded, liked working for someone he believed he could control. Neither Sandy nor the boss objected to the frequent clashes. Both worked off steam during the confrontations and never had any bad feelings afterward.

Eventually, a vice president to whom Sandy's boss reported became concerned about the well-known battles between Sandy and his boss. He called Sandy's boss on the carpet and told him to stop the battling immediately and to fire Sandy if he could not be restrained. Thereafter, Sandy's boss sought support from other employees in the department and lost interest in Sandy.

Because of the abrupt change in his relationship with his boss, Sandy felt that he had "sounded off once too often." He suspected that his boss was getting ready to fire him. As a result, he started looking for another job, and his interest in his current job declined. His boss became aware of the decline in performance and confronted Sandy with it. That final confrontation led to immediate dismissal.

DECISION POINTS

While the turnover process may vary considerably in duration, the pattern is the same. Typically, in an employee's work history there are four critical decision points (see Figure 10):

1. Postorientation.
2. Satisfaction (periodic checks).
3. Changes in relationships.
4. Warnings (heeded or unheeded).

Let's reexamine Beth's case more closely to see how the turnover process develops.

At the very onset of the process, Beth made an unfavorable *postorientation* decision. She perceived the work environment to be restrictive for women who had management aspirations. Thus pressure to leave the organization began to build. At this point, counseling by her supervisor or members of the personnel staff might have dispelled her unfavorable feelings. But since Beth presented no problems and appeared to like the organization and her job, no one initiated a career dialogue.

Thereafter, she periodically reassessed her *satisfaction* with her job and the work environment. As long as she continued to feel that she was growing personally and moving in a forward direction, she decided to stay with the company. However, at the five-year mark she decided that she had reached a point where her future progress was blocked.

In just five years, she felt she was "topping out." Her feelings were triggered by the failure of high-performing women colleagues to get promotions when openings occurred. She commiserated with the passed-over colleagues, reinforcing her negative feelings about the opportunities for women in the company.

Adding to the pressure to withdraw from the company

Figure 10. Turnover process.

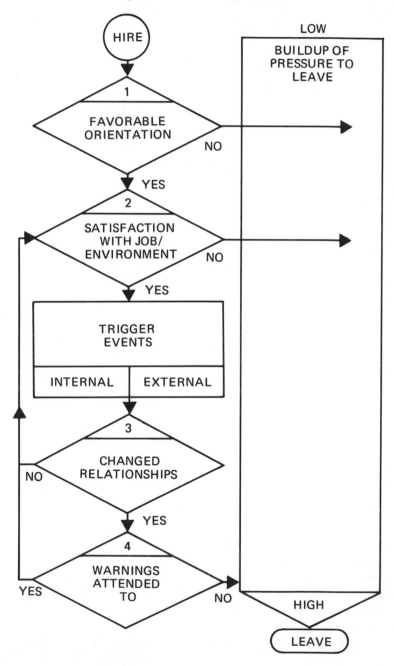

were external events. In the trade press, Beth read of women with comparable credentials who were progressing in their companies. And in a businesswomen's organization that she belonged to, she talked with women who appeared to be progressing faster than she was, and was told of available opportunities for which she was well qualified.

As she moved toward an inevitable resignation, her dissatisfaction grew. But no one in the organization talked to her about her concerns. Thus she couldn't rid herself of the feelings that were making her increasingly unhappy with the organization.

Despite the fact that her supervisors and colleagues were "surprised" when she decided to leave, Beth had issued many *warnings* during her late career stages. She had asked her supervisor why some of the top female performers had been passed over for promotion. He had been evasive in explaining what had happened and appeared to be unwilling to confront the real issue. At her annual performance appraisal, her supervisor gave a once-over-lightly treatment to the career-planning section of the appraisal form.

Beth had even visited the personnel department to discuss future growth opportunities. She was supplied with some general information. But her concerns about the limited opportunities for female managers were brushed aside with the abrupt statement, "We are an equal opportunity organization."

Thus the turnover process led to the loss of an outstanding performer and valuable human resource. Warnings had been ignored, and repeated opportunities for intervention, which would have aborted the process, were not recognized.

CRITICAL TRIGGER EVENTS

From the very start of employment, employees ask themselves two key questions:

Is this a good job?

Is this an organization I want to continue to work for?

The answers to these questions change significantly after critical trigger events. Managers who are alert to events that are likely to trigger a change in an employee's feelings are in a better position to intervene. They can prepare the employee for subsequent disappointment and can offer support thereafter.

Certainly, managers should expect problems when the following common events occur:

Passed Over for Promotion

A missed promotional opportunity is often viewed as the "end of the line." Employees may believe they have been labeled nonpromotable. Disappointed and angry, and concerned about what others may think, they may feel the only way to save face is to leave the organization.

Inadequate Merit Increase

Employees, particularly high performers, believe their value to an organization is directly proportional to the merit increase they receive. If there is a significant difference between what they think they should be getting and what they actually get, they will become dissatisfied. Unfortunately, their expectations may be unrealistic, particularly when they are uninformed about compensation policy in their own and other organizations.

Conflict

Although a few employees thrive on conflict, most employees are troubled by it, particularly if they are the losers in conflict situations. Depending on how seriously they perceive the loss, employees may feel that the work environment has become intolerable.

Significant Changes

It's natural to resist change. However, when change is perceived as threatening, employees may seek relief by

withdrawing from the situation. Reorganization, reassignment, relocation—any form of "starting over again"—is
viewed with trepidation by many employees.

New Frame of Reference

When something happens that forces an employee to re-
assess what he wants from his job, contentment may
rapidly become discontentment. For example, a single employee gets married, and her outlook about the job
changes. An employee who has been pursuing education
at night graduates with an advanced degree and feels that
he wants to use his new skills in a higher-level job. Or a
dramatic personal event, like a death of a spouse or a di-
vorce, changes an employee's frame of reference and
makes the job less desirable.

If managers fail to notice these key trigger events, they
may get a "second chance" if they are able to recognize
the warning signals that commonly follow such events.
Employees reacting to trigger events begin to see only
negatives in the work environment, overlooking any positives. The smallest things bother them. They tend to dis-
associate themselves from the organization, assuming the
role of uninvolved critic. They gripe continually and seek
the comfort of other gripers. Perhaps this description
sounds familiar to you:

"Charlie used to be a quiet, uncomplaining guy. I don't
know why, but he sure has changed. At staff meetings
he continually makes sarcastic remarks about things the
department is doing. Or he makes some wisecracks under his breath to a colleague next to him. He's not deliberately uncooperative, but he certainly couldn't be
called cooperative: he wouldn't go one inch out of his
way to help somebody else. And he doesn't seem to be
willing to share even the good things that happen. He
used to be fairly popular in the department, but his sul-
lenness has turned off everyone except a small group of
malcontents who pal around together."

The employee's change in attitude is the beginning of a downward spiral. The employee's energy wanes, his judgment is impaired, and he becomes uninvolved, uncommitted, and eventually uncaring about the quality of his performance.

Sometimes the performance change occurs so rapidly that it demands the manager's attention. However, more often it happens gradually, and unless the manager is sensitive, it may go unnoticed until it reaches a serious, perhaps irreversible stage. Here's how one manager described changes in a subordinate's behavior:

"About a week after her performance appraisal, I noticed a change in the way Debbie was acting. She was slightly cooler in her relationship with me: she smiled less often and appeared to be less willing to talk. In group activities, she was somewhat more withdrawn, limiting her participation and staying on the edge of discussions. Small errors began to creep into her usually letter-perfect reports. Something was wrong—not one big thing I could discuss with her, but a whole series of little things."

A common indication of someone turning off on the job after a trigger event is increased involvement in outside activities. Perhaps the employee starts attending more trade association meetings, where she can make new employment contacts. Or an employee may increase his out-of-office activities, such as calling on customers and suppliers, to gain an opportunity to make side trips to employment agencies or prospective employers. Often an employee will visit casually with the personnel department and ask about a transfer. Or he may drop into other departments to inquire informally about possible openings.

As employees decide to leave, their behavioral patterns reveal an increasing dissatisfaction with the job and the company. The manager who is alert to these warning signs can anticipate developing problems and intervene before they get out of hand. Rarely is there any justification for a manager being "surprised" by an employee's termination.

COMMONSENSE ACTIONS

1. Develop your own list of trigger events and a system for keeping close track of how employees are likely to be affected by such events. For example, any performance appraisal that appears to be poorly received should be placed in a special alert folder. I use a red folder to remind me of the urgency of the need to follow up.

2. When you observe a change in an employee's behavior, start a *diary of events*. It will help you become aware of "a lot of little things" happening. And when you ultimately confront the employee, instead of discussing vague feelings that you have, you can refer to specific events, times, and places.

3. Schedule *regular* job counseling sessions with employees. Your objective during these sessions is to demonstrate your interest in the employee and to encourage openness in discussing job satisfaction.

4. Confront employees whenever you suspect that they are becoming dissatisfied with their jobs and getting ready psychologically to leave. Your objective in talking with them is to help them overcome their tunnel vision. For example, after five years in the job a valued employee in the research and development department of a large pharmaceuticals company began to feel that he had a limited future. Soon afterward, a colleague with comparable qualifications left the company for a better-paying, more responsible job. The colleague's resignation triggered an upsurge of negative feelings in the employee. His supervisor recognized what was happening and called him in for a counseling session:

SUPERVISOR I get the feeling that you're not as happy in the job as you used to be.

EMPLOYEE Why do you say that?

SUPERVISOR (*Referring to his own log of recent events*) Here are just some of the observations I've made recently.

EMPLOYEE (*After listening to the observations*) I guess you really have been watching me closely.

SUPERVISOR I'm interested in you. You're a valued employee and I hope that, after the number of years we've worked together, you are also a good friend.

EMPLOYEE I'm sorry. I'm not angry at you, but I am beginning to become concerned about my status in this company. (*The employee goes on to explain, with some coaxing from his supervisor, the sources of his frustration.*)

SUPERVISOR I can appreciate how you feel. And I can understand why you are considering looking for another job. That may be the right thing for you to do, or it may not be. Let's evaluate the pros and cons of the situation. I'll try to be as objective as I can. Naturally, I have a bias—I want you to stay. But I want you to stay only if it's right for you. Otherwise you won't be happy. (*The supervisor helps the employee realistically assess the situation. He doesn't pressure him to stay. Instead, he tries to help the employee explore his career status more fully.*)

5. Consider the human side of your plans. Your actions often affect employees who work for you and with you. Inadvertently, through a seemingly harmless action, you may trigger negative feelings in an employee. Had you realized the consequences, you might not have taken the action, or you might have done things differently.

6. Fortunately, the decision to leave an organization builds over time. You will be more successful in retaining valued employees if you intervene in the process as early as possible. To do so, you have to be continually concerned about the job satisfaction of your employees and must stay alert to early signs of deterioration in job satisfaction.

CHAPTER 7

Reasons for Leaving

WHEN examining the carefully compiled turnover statistics of clients, I always ask this question:

"How legitimate are the recorded reasons for leaving?"

The question provokes defensiveness and an elaborate justification of the impressive tables and graphs. I listen patiently and then ask:

"But how do you decide in which category to classify a termination?"

By now, the defensiveness of the client has changed to impatience and I get this condescending reply:

"The resigning employee or terminating manager tells us."

That's an overly simple answer to a very complex question.

Employees and manager might "tell you" if they were willing to discuss the subject. They could provide direct answers if they themselves knew. Certainly, if they didn't have anything to hide, they would be willing to discuss fully their reasons for leaving. And they might be frank if they felt that there was no risk in being candid and some benefit in doing so.

Unfortunately, the resigning employee or terminating manager usually doesn't want to tell all, doesn't really know, has something to hide, and feels that the risks involved in being candid outweigh the benefits. That's why the real story behind neatly classified reasons for leaving may conflict with recorded data.

THE "PAT" REASONS FOR LEAVING

To demonstrate the critical differences between recorded and real reasons, let's examine four case histories:

Lou's resignation was recorded as "left for another job." This is a catchall classification that provides little insight into why an employee resigns. In reality, Lou didn't leave for another job; he left to escape his current job. For over seven years, he had been a customer services manager. Each day he spent virtually all his time handling complaints, usually with a telephone glued to his ear.

Lou did his job well and was experienced enough to cope with even the loudest and rudest customers; nevertheless, some customers penetrated his armor and inflicted daily pain. According to him, the punishments of the job were much greater than the rewards. The standard annual merit increase, modest compensation, and rare "pat on the back" couldn't offset the daily battering he got from his customers.

Yet the only explanation he gave to his boss when he

resigned was, "I have enjoyed working with you and the company and I like my job, but I just got an offer I couldn't refuse."

Rosalyn left for a convenient, no-fault reason. According to the official records, she decided to "stay home." Although she had worked hard to become a competent computer programmer, she apparently decided to become a homemaker and perhaps start a family.

Because her husband had a good job, Rosalyn did not have to remain in a career she no longer enjoyed. Instead, she could leave immediately and take her time looking for another job. She preferred to cover up her real reasons for leaving because she didn't want a confrontation. Her escape was painless.

The real issue was a nonsupportive supervisor. Rosalyn described him as a "carbon copy of my father." Rosalyn's father had demanded top performance from her, reminding her of any shortcomings but rarely acknowledging her successes. On the job, her boss followed the same pattern. Although Rosalyn performed outstandingly and her boss had high regard for her, she felt she was unable to please him. She was hesitant to share her problems with him, fearing that he would interpret them as signs of weakness.

For about two years, Rosalyn harbored feelings of dissatisfaction. Her only confidant was her husband, and eventually he became concerned about her dissatisfaction, which was affecting their family life. It was natural for him to suggest, "Why don't you just quit, and look for another job? We don't need the money. Why put up with all that aggravation?"

She acted on her husband's suggestion in a week. He had proposed what she had been thinking about for quite some time.

Warren officially left "for more money." In an inflationary economy, "leaving for money" is often a legitimate
reason, yet it may represent only a superficial explanation. Warren was a high achiever. For each of the five
years he worked for the company, he was one of the
"top salesmen of the year." In all the sales contests in
which he participated, he was either a winner or a close
runner-up. Yet Warren felt that he was not being recognized for his achievement. His merit increases were only
"somewhat" greater than the merit increases of mediocre performers. His commissions were greater than
those of most of the other sales representatives in the
company. But according to Warren, the "spread" between what he received and what mediocre performers
received wasn't sufficient.

Compensation represented recognition for Warren.
While he left the organization ostensibly because he
wanted more money, in reality he was leaving because
he believed he was not getting recognition.

Bernie was dismissed because of "inability to perform
the job." Although he had worked for the company for
ten years, he had been on his job for only six months
before his dismissal. There was no question that Bernie's
performance was unacceptable. But he wasn't incapable
of doing the job, and he was beginning to "learn the
ropes" when he was dismissed.

Unfortunately, he was the victim of a nonresponsive and
nonsupportive supervisor. Previously, he had been a
technician in the research and development laboratories.
Then top management initiated a program of job rotation, and Bernie was forced upon the marketing department. The transition would have been difficult enough
under ordinary circumstances, because he had no background in marketing. But his transition became an or-
deal because he had to work in a hostile environment.
He received minimal instruction. His colleagues were

uncooperative. His supervisor was an adversary rather than a helper. And all the people around him acted as if they were just waiting for him to fail.

Eventually, he did fail, and in the process the new system of job rotation failed as well.

In all four of these cases, the "pat" reasons for leaving were whitewashed, covering up the real reasons.

THE REAL REASONS FOR LEAVING

Usually, employers accept without question uncontrollable reasons for leaving, such as marriage, pregnancy, poor health, relocation, return to school, and starting one's own business. However, these uncontrollable reasons may have been "no hassle" ways of explaining a resignation. The woman who leaves a dissatisfying career for marriage or a homemaker's role may have deliberately created her escape route. The employee who returns to school, decides to move to another city, or retires early may also be withdrawing from an unpleasant work environment.

Employees contribute to the whitewash, because they fool themselves, want to hide their real reasons, or feel there is no payoff and a possible penalty in a full disclosure. They cover up deliberately to avoid embarrassing exposure of personal deficiencies: inability to adapt, learning difficulties, lack of competitiveness, interpersonal problems, or technical obsolescence.

Usually, employees whitewash their reasons because it makes sense to "keep your mouth shut." Complete honesty may have a flood of consequences, as it did for this middle-aged executive:

"Foolishly, I resigned without lining up a new job first. I worked for a supervisor who was eventually fired because of his incompetence. He was making a complete mess of our department. Before I left, I tried to warn management about what was happening, but my warnings were discounted as personal bias. Thereafter, because I had been outspoken, I received bad references from the company, which hindered my subsequent job search."

Employers are equally guilty of whitewashing. They deceive themselves or deliberately cover up embarrassments. Supervisors prefer not to disclose their managerial deficiencies, and organizations choose to ignore inequities in their policies and procedures. It's easier to pin the blame on an employee, sidestepping responsibility for a resignation or termination.

The consequences of accepting less than legitimate reasons for leaving are serious. Human resources are wasted, at considerable expense. And the problems that led to the waste of human resources remain unresolved. Whenever I investigate the turnover of an organization, I discover that management has an unrealistic understanding of its turnover problem—self-deception distorts management's point of view.

A company cannot manage its valuable human resources intelligently without an accurate assessment of why employees leave. If management accepts less than legitimate reasons for turnover, it is virtually impossible to confront the problem.

COMMONSENSE ACTIONS

1. In addition to the commonly employed separation interview, a follow-up program is highly desirable. About six weeks after an employee leaves, he or she should be sent a letter asking for comments on the reasons for the separation. If possible, the letter should be addressed from the office of the president and should ask for comments on company policies and procedures rather than on specific individuals.

2. A variation of this technique is to supply the separated employee with a suspense-date letter, to be returned whenever the employee feels he or she wants to offer additional comments or request a postemployment hearing.

3. One of the most significant things managers can do is to assume a measure of personal fault in every separation and try to learn what they may have done wrong. Managers must accept whatever employees tell them without becoming defensive, and in the spirit of avoiding a repetition of their errors.

4. In addition to compiling turnover statistics, you should summarize key background data relevant to a separation. The following format is recommended:

- Employee's stated reason for leaving.
- Other factors that may have contributed to employee's dissatisfaction.
- Willingness and openness of the employee to discuss reasons for separation.
- Personal relationship between employee and supervisor.
- Attitude of the employee toward the company.

5. Develop a separation kit. In addition to the usual personnel information, describing how to continue medical coverage and other items, include an audiotape containing a set of instructions from personnel. In effect, it should be a self-conducted post-employment interview to be completed by the separating employee in the privacy of his home. It asks him to answer questions about why he is leaving the organization. It explains how to answer the questions fully, and tries to impress him with the importance of sharing that information. The kit should also include a postemployment interview form with a suspense date.

If possible, obtain professional help in preparing the audiotape. The personnel department can often be of assistance. If you want to develop your own audiotape, you might use the following outline as a guide:

OUTLINE FOR SEPARATION AUDIOTAPE

1. A discussion of the importance and benefits of sharing candid information about the reasons for leaving an organization.

2. A guarantee of confidentiality and protection from any negative consequences arising from sharing the information.

3. Requests for information on the following subjects:
   Supervision
   Work environment
   Work assignment
   Pay and benefits
   Promotion
   Growth

4. An inquiry into the circumstances under which the employee would be willing to return to the organization.

5. Solicitation of suggestions for improvements in any of the areas described in question 3.

6. A general discussion of the need to supply specific supporting evidence for opinions and attitudes.

CHAPTER 8

Turnover Costs

EVERYBODY knows turnover is expensive. But it's an expense that is accepted without question until it reaches serious proportions. Then someone says, "Do you have any idea how much turnover is costing us?"

Many organizations don't know what turnover costs, and individual managers rarely bear financial responsibility for it. The reason is that turnover costs are not quantified and fiscal responsibility isn't assigned. Turnover costs reach alarming levels before managers pay attention to them, and the cumulative bottom-line impact on the organization reaches an embarrassing magnitude.

What appears to be a sweep-under-the-rug attitude about turnover costs is, in reality, an inadequate system of control. Managers measure only selected turnover costs, usually the extremely clear-cut and easy-to-quantify costs, and ignore other critical costs that take special effort to calculate.

Evaluation and control of turnover costs requires a full understanding of relevant cost components, tangible and intangible, and the systematic collection of data in a form that can be understood and interpreted by managers. This approach will make managers more aware of the expense of turnover and enable them to budget for and control turnover costs more effectively.

The principal cost elements of turnover may be divided into two categories: those that are tangible or measurable and those that are intangible or relatively unmeasurable. Both categories of costs can have a major impact on the organization.

TANGIBLE COSTS

The major tangible costs of turnover can be subdivided into the costs of recruitment, selection, orientation and training, and separation.

Recruitment

When managers are personally responsible for finding new employees, they are much more aware of the cost of advertising and/or employment agency fees. However, many organizations, particularly large ones, provide managers with staff assistance in generating a supply of candidates. The cost of this assistance may or may not be directly assigned, in full or in part, to the manager's budget. In addition, organizations often maintain an ongoing college recruiting program which is usually considered part of "fixed" overhead.

Internal recruitment—identifying candidates within the organization—is usually overlooked as a turnover cost, and certainly is not charged back to the manager. Also, in trying to attract candidates, organizations may make heavy investments in brochures, pamphlets, and public relations activities. And, to encourage employees to seek out friends or acquaintances as possible candidates, many organizations establish bounty systems for recommendations that lead to employment. The manager gets a "free ride" on all these costs.

Thus there are direct and indirect recruitment costs which should be specifically chargeable as expenses.

Selection

One of the major costs of selection is the time spent by staff and line personnel in interviewing candidates. Usually this cost is treated as a fixed expense. However, the number of people interviewed and the amount of time spent interviewing vary widely.

Expenses associated with recruiting and processing applicants can also be considerable. These include travel expenses (particularly when the applicant is flown in from a distance), psychological tests, and preemployment medical examinations. In addition, while visiting the company, an applicant often tours the facility, expending the time of a guide and each person the applicant talks to. After the candidate leaves, line and personnel staff usually conduct reference checks and/or credit and security checks. All these "time" costs add to the total burden.

Finally, throughout the selection process, a considerable amount of correspondence may be exchanged. Extensive paperwork is required. The cost of the printed forms and the processing of these forms contribute further to the overhead burden.

Many of these selection costs are either overlooked or allocated as part of overall personnel overhead—yet the expenses are controllable and measurable.

Orientation and Training

Breaking in a new employee entails significant costs. Depending on the complexity of the job, both formal and on-the-job training may be required. Often, the supervisor will have to work closely with the new employee, and the assistance of co-workers may be necessary.

While the employee is "learning the ropes," the quantity and quality of his or her performance is usually substandard. Therefore, there are associated quality control, scrap, and maintenance costs.

While virtually all organizations recognize that the new employee costs more to maintain than the employee already on staff, they usually don't keep track of the direct and indirect expenses incurred. A prevailing attitude is, "The costs of breaking in an employee are unavoidable. Why should we keep track of every penny, particularly when people will be paid a salary whether they spend the time breaking in the employee or working at their regular assignments?"

However, "watched" activities tend to be more efficient. When there is a lack of accountability, there is usually less incentive to avoid waste.

Separation

The costs of separating employees, particularly long-term employees, can be extremely high. Often, the amount of severance pay is directly related to the amount of guilt the employer feels in terminating the employee. For example, when a long-term employee is separated because he was moved into a assignment that "didn't work out," some companies may give him as much as six months to a year of severance pay.

In addition, extra social security tax and unemployment insurance contributions must be borne by the employer because of turnover. The employer ceases to make a tax contribution on the wages or salaries of each of its employees when the annual Social Security limit is reached. But when new employees are hired, these Social Security tax payments must be continued.

There are time costs as well—the time spent by personnel representatives and others involved in separation processing and exit interviewing. In some cases, the amount of time devoted to these activities can be considerable.

Other costs are incurred because of the understaffing resulting from turnover. There may be a production loss and unfilled orders due to the vacancy. Overtime and temporary help may be required. In a manufacturing plant, there may be idle machinery.

Most of these separation costs, with the exception of separation pay, aren't calculated. That's because few companies have systems for collecting the data they need to accurately assign a dollar value to these costs.

INTANGIBLE COSTS

In addition to the tangible costs described, there are intangible costs that are hard to measure but that nevertheless have considerable financial impact on the organization.

High on the list of intangible costs is the disruption of morale resulting from turnover. Employees who stay with an organization are very interested in the reasons colleagues leave the organization. Perhaps they feel they are victims of the same problems but have not been able to "work up the courage" to leave. Additional turnover may arise because of this process of identification. Employees feel, "I'm in the same situation, and if they can escape by finding a better job, so can I."

Even when employees don't have the same concerns as employees who have left, they are affected by their loss. Their work demands may increase as a result of the vacancy, and they may be forced to work overtime in order to fulfill the duties of the employee who has left.

Another disruption caused by the loss of an employee is the breakdown of work teams. Perhaps the employee was a formal or informal leader of the team or a skilled team worker. She may have supplied the "glue" that kept the group together and maintained its smooth functioning.

When the group reached an impasse, the employee may have been the one who always suggested a compromise; or when group members started choosing sides in a conflict, she may have been a natural mediator. Perhaps the employee served as the "idea man," stimulating the thinking of the group when others had tunnel vision.

Besides the loss of team leadership resulting from the departure of a key employee, a loss of department leadership may occur because the supervisor becomes preoccupied with recruiting, selecting, orienting, and training a replacement. The supervisor may become unavailable to staff members who need his guidance and support.

Finally, a loss of employees has *external* impact on the organization. Perhaps the departing employees had special rapport with customers. Often, customer relationships are fragile, and the loss of a key employee can lead to the loss of a major customer. Also, when an organization lays off personnel, there may be a loss of goodwill in the community, with long-range impact on the company's reputation.

These intangible costs hurt the organization, disrupting it and indirectly creating economic costs. Yet few organizations attempt to measure and monitor these costs.

COMMONSENSE ACTIONS

1. Using the checklist shown in Figure 11, take an inventory of which turnover costs in your organization are currently being accounted for. Once the inventory is completed, consider ways in which you might collect data on some of the areas that are currently being overlooked. For example, you can certainly account for the time you spend in recruitment, selection, orientation, training, and separation. The time sheet shown in Figure 12 can help you keep track of these activities. You may be reluctant to take on the extra paperwork, but a study tracking the costs of just one terminated employee should convince you otherwise. These costs often reach alarming proportions.

2. When turnover costs are monitored regularly, the organization is in a better position to assign accountability and to develop benchmarks for budgeting. (See Figure 13.) Turnover persists in an organization when managers do not feel responsible for its expense. If managers are given budgeting responsibility, they are more likely to become aware of how they contribute to mounting turnover costs and to take steps to reduce these costs.

Since the organization's vitality depends on the flow of people in and out, turnover costs can't be eliminated. But they can be monitored and controlled, adding substantial amounts to the bottom line of the profit-and-loss statement.

Figure 11. Checklist of turnover costs.

	Charged	Not Charged
I. *Tangible Costs*		
1. *Recruitment*		
(a) Job specification		
(b) Advertising		
(c) College recruitment		
(d) Employment agency		
(e) Prizes and awards		
(f) Literature		
(g) Correspondence		
2. *Selection*		
(a) Interviewing		
(b) Testing		
(c) Medical exam		
(d) Reference checks		
(e) Processing applications		
(f) Credit and security checks		
(g) Travel costs		
(h) Tours		
(i) Forms		
(j) Correspondence		

	Charged	Not Charged
3. *Orientation*		
(a) By supervision		
(b) By staff		
(c) By co-workers		
4. *Training*		
(a) Formal		
by staff		
by external suppliers		
(b) On-the-job		
by supervision		
by co-workers		
5. *Production*		
(a) Substandard production		
(b) Reduced production		
(c) Quality control costs		
(d) Wastage costs		
(e) Overtime		
6. *Separation*		
(a) Severance pay		
(b) Extra social security and unemployment payments		
(c) Exit interviews		
7. *Vacancy*		
(a) Overtime		
(b) Temporary help		
(c) Idle machinery		
(d) Unfilled orders		
II. *Intangible Costs*		
1. Disruption of morale		
2. Stimulation of additional turnover		
3. Workload demands		
4. Goodwill and reputation		
5. Team disruption		
6. Preoccupation of supervision in orientation and training		
7. Creation of feelings of insecurity		

Figure 12. Turnover time sheet.

ACTIVITY	DATE	TIME
Recruitment		
Selection		
Orientation		
Training		
Separation		

Figure 13. Quarterly turnover report.

Manager _____

Department _____ Date _____

	Current Qtr.	Last Yr./Qtr.	Curr. Yr. to Date	Last Yr. to Date
I. *Number of employees*				
Quits				
Dismissals				
Layoffs				
Other				
Total				
Turnover rate				

Figure 13. Quarterly turnover report (continued).

	Current Quarter		Year to Date	
	Budget	Actual	Budget	Actual
II. *Costs*				
Recruitment				
Selection				
Orientation				
Training				
Separation				
Production				
Total				

PART TWO

SYMPTOMS OF
UNDERLYING
PROBLEMS

A physician diagnoses an illness by recognizing symptoms. In the same way, you can diagnose poor health in
your organization by recognizing the underlying problems
associated with turnover.

For example, "sick" selection policies and procedures
may result in the hiring of underqualified or overqualified
employees who become increasingly dissatisfied with a job
in which they are misplaced. Recognition of the association between turnover and faulty selection policies leads
to improvement in the selection process and, ultimately, to
control of turnover.

In this part of the book, we will take a close look at the
major areas in which managerial missteps can precipitate
turnover. These include employee selection, work assignment, pay and benefits, promotion, supervision, work environment, and employee development. You may feel that
these key areas already get regular attention from management. But have you looked at them from the eyes of de-

parting employees? What you see as smooth-functioning policies and procedures may appear to be unjust or inadequate to your subordinates. Understanding their frame of reference can help you define areas that need improvement and can help you change their perspective if necessary.

Once you recognize turnover as a symptom of underlying problems, you can begin to search for patterns of poor health within the organization. When these patterns are uncovered, you can do something about them, strengthening the organization and controlling turnover.

CHAPTER 9

Selection Problems

COMPANIES repeatedly make the same hiring mistakes. They select people who are likely to fail. Or they select people who are unlikely to stay with the organization. In either case, the selection process contributes substantially to turnover problems.

Naturally, managers do not intentionally make hiring mistakes. But by failing to see how selection procedures relate to turnover problems, managers are doomed to repeat their errors. For example, the director of a large sales force attributed heavy turnover to what he thought was "below average" compensation. Yet compensation surveys indicated that the sales force was paid competitively.

After studying exit interview data from the company

and talking to key personnel, I discovered that the turn-over problem resulted from "overhiring." Most of the new sales representatives were MBA graduates with top scholastic records. They were highly ambitious, upwardly mobile employees who became discontented with the job after a relatively short period of time.

COMMON DEFICIENCIES IN THE SELECTION PROCESS

Each of the following deficiencies in the selection process can lead to turnover problems.

Inadequate Job Specification

Many organizations routinely prepare job specifications that have no value. The specifications may be obsolete, unrealistic, or unclear. Few managers take the time to think about the kinds of employees who are likely to be successful in and satisfied with a specific job. They focus on attributes unrelated to job success and overlook necessary qualifications. For example, a job specification may call for specialized experience. Yet the systems and procedures in the company may be so unique that previous experience is of no consequence. On the other hand, the job may be such that the employee has to work alone virtually all the time. Yet the job specification doesn't call for someone who has demonstrated an ability to work alone and who enjoys a solitary occupation.

Failure to Document Selection Mistakes

Of course, managers want to forget their hiring mistakes. But there is usually something to be learned from them. Whenever it becomes obvious that the wrong person was put into a job, either because the employee was unsuited for it or because the employee really didn't want to hold the job, at least for a reasonable period of time, the manager should try to answer these questions:

○ What did I overlook during the selection process that might have made me see that hiring this employee was questionable?

○ In specifying the qualifications for this job, did I understate or overstate them?

○ Did I overlook any important selection criteria?

Hiring "Warm" Bodies

When it is difficult to recruit candidates and there is pressure to fill a job quickly, managers often lower their job qualifications and assume a high risk by hiring marginal candidates. The employees may be "warm" when hired, but they turn "cold" immediately thereafter. For example:

A manager of marketing research needed an assistant with experience in questionnaire design, interviewing, and statistics. Perhaps because the job paid only a junior's salary, the manager had difficulty attracting candidates. After a fruitless search for three months, he decided to hire a promising beginner whom he would train. Unfortunately, the workload was very heavy and the manager found that he had little time for training. The new employee was forced to teach himself the job. Although he tried hard and was able to learn some aspects of the job, he made serious mistakes that were directly attributable to his lack of experience. His subsequent failure was predictable—and could have been avoided.

Emphasis on Factors Unrelated to Performance

Many managers hire stereotypes. They select candidates who "look good." Height, weight, age, school attended, social affiliations, and other criteria unrelated to performance are assigned undue importance. For example, in working with a problem unit at one company, I got the uncomfortable feeling that the manager of the unit was hiring clones. There was a remarkable similarity in appearance and background between the manager and his

subordinates. When I questioned him about these sim-
ilarities, he supplied an elaborate justification. The turnover problem in the unit wasn't resolved until the
manager changed his selection criteria, focusing instead
on performance-related characteristics.

Reliance on Tests

Certainly, objective, valid data are welcome in any selection process. But the data should not serve as a substitute
for judgment. Usually, tests do not differentiate well
among qualified candidates. And some essential qualities
in job applicants just cannot be tested. Yet managers will
commonly say:

> "I've really hired a winner. Her test scores were over
> 85."

> "I have two qualified candidates for the job. I'm going to
> hire the one with the higher scores."

Unrealistic Job Expectations

Employees often accept a job with a mistaken impression of what the job entails. And they are subsequently
disappointed when the job doesn't meet their expectations.
Often, the problem is that the manager failed to supply a
complete description of the job, particularly its less ap-
pealing aspects. For example, a young lawyer with outstanding credentials accepted a position on the legal staff
of a leading corporation. He believed that he would be
given an opportunity to use his full capabilities, particularly his specialized legal training. Instead, he performed menial activities that he thought a legal clerk
could easily do.

Hiring Candidates Who Interview Well

Managers often hire candidates on the basis of superficial first impressions. They are fooled by glib candidates
who present themselves well in interviews. But proficiency in interviewing isn't related to performance.

Ignoring Risk Factors

Candidates tell interviewers, "I am a high risk," but the warning goes unheeded. That's because the message is usually expressed indirectly rather than directly. For example, a candidate may say, "I have planned my career carefully. I know exactly where I want to go and how long it should take me to get there." In effect, the candidate is warning the potential employer that any barrier to her career plans, or delays in the timetable, may lead to unrest and a job change. Or a candidate may say, "I have lived in this community all my life; so has my wife. We really have roots here." If the new employer has any plans to move the employee in the future, the employee may seek a new job.

Job candidates reveal their feelings about the kind of work they enjoy—and the kind of job and company in which they would be content—to managers who listen carefully and know how to interpret the meaning behind the candidates' statements.

Shortchanging the Time Invested in Selection

Many managers consider the time invested in selection an extra burden on an already overburdened workload. They reluctantly "fit in" time for developing job specifications, interviewing, and carrying out the other steps in the selection process. Often, when they participate in these selection activities, their minds are elsewhere.

By shortchanging the time invested in the selection process, managers seriously compromise the quality of their hiring decisions. For example, one large clinical laboratory was concerned about its alarming turnover rate. The root of the problem was that the supervisory staff had an extremely heavy workload. As a result, the supervisors had to use their personal time to recruit and interview new employees. Naturally, the supervisors were reluctant to sacrifice too much of their time, so they abbreviated all the steps in the selection process, compromising its effectiveness.

Limited Shopping

Many managers, particularly very busy managers, feel that they cannot afford to spend time shopping around for the right candidate. They work with a limited number of recruitment sources and generally see only a handful of candidates. By doing so, they narrow their choices and increase the chances of making a mistake.

Selection depends on sufficient numbers. For example, you may have to screen anywhere from 20 to 50 résumés to find 10 candidates with the qualifications you're seeking. Thereafter, telephone interviewing may cut the list of candidates in half. Subsequent in-person interviewing will further narrow the choice of qualified candidates.

There are many areas in which managers are prone to making selection errors. And these selection errors are directly related to turnover problems.

COMMONSENSE ACTIONS

By strengthening the selection process, you can help to reduce turnover. Each of the following commonsense actions can improve selection procedures.

1. In developing a job specification, use the existing job description as the starting point, not the end point. Ask yourself, "What kind of person is likely to be most qualified and most content in performing the duties outlined in the job description?" Try to identify with incoming employees and consider who they will be working with, how they will spend their time, and what challenges and problems they may encounter. Pay particular attention to any aspect of the job or work environment that could create problems for the new employee. By identifying with the new employee, you are in a better position to understand his or her wants and needs and to develop a profile of the kind of person who is most likely to succeed.

2. Once you have found someone you feel is qualified to work for your organization, make certain that the job is right for the candidate. Unfortunately, managers tend to

oversell a job to potential employees, and the potential employees are so intent on trying to sell themselves that they don't pay sufficient attention to how well the job suits them.

Candidates should be given a realistic job orientation. Ideally, managers should schedule a *work preview*, giving potential employees an opportunity to see what the job is really like. For example, one company invites qualified sales candidates to spend a day in the field working with a sales representative. Several candidates have declined the job after this work preview because they realized that it was not what they wanted.

3. The subjectivity that interferes with making an accurate assessment of candidates can be offset by scheduling multiple interviews. When several different people evaluate a candidate and then get together to reconcile their points of view, the final evaluation is much more accurate than when only one person interviews the candidate.

4. To avoid "cloning," try to identify, in writing, the stereotyped characteristics you ordinarily seek in new employees. Review the list before each interview, and ask yourself continually during the interview, "Am I really evaluating the candidate, or responding to a stereotype?"

5. Make certain that you allocate sufficient time to each step of the selection process. Rushing the process increases your chance of making an error. The extra time you invest in selection will be worth it.

6. After the first few minutes of an interview, briefly note your first impressions of the candidate in writing. These first impressions can distort your subsequent evaluation of the candidate. By bringing them to light, you will reduce their potency. For example, after a few minutes you may note, "This candidate comes on strong; he appears to be brash and makes me uncomfortable." Thereafter, you will be better able to question your feelings. ("Am I objectively evaluating the candidate's qualifications, or am I allowing my negative first impressions to influence me?")

Figure 14. Weights to be assigned to information from application form.

(CIRCLE THE APPROPRIATE NUMBER)

	Neutral or Negative Factors	Moderately Positive Factors	Strongly Positive Factors
Months at present address	Less than 75 +1	75 to 150 +2	150 or more +3
Education	Did not graduate high school +3	Graduated high school +6	Some college or graduated +12
Service citations	Two or more +5	Only one +10	None +15
Past compensation	Salary only or commission only +3	Salary and commission +6	Salary and bonus +12
Previous experience	No sales +5	Other sales +10	Pharm. sales +15
Months self-employed	Less than 6 months +2	6 months to 1 year +10	More than 1 year +15
Value of house	Less than $50,000 +4	$50,000 to $80,000 +8	Over $80,000 +15

Sum _____   Sum _____   Sum _____

Grand Total _____

SCORING

Negative   Any score below 42 is an indication that further processing of the applicant is unlikely to produce fruitful results.

Moderately Positive   Any score in the 43–60 range is an indication that further processing could well yield worthwhile results.

Strongly Positive   Any score above 60 is a very positive indication that further processing is worthwhile.

7. A weighted application blank can be helpful in "red flagging" aspects of a candidate's background. The weights are determined by evaluating the backgrounds of known high and low performers. You may be able to assign weights informally by eyeballing the application blanks or you may wish to obtain the assistance of a statistician to derive weightings based on multiple correlation methods. Figure 14 illustrates one weighted application system for a pharmaceuticals sales representative.

8. For each job title under your supervision, ask the current title holder to prepare a job specification to supplement the traditional job description. Keep both on file.

9. A final commonsense action that has special significance is to *challenge* every hire. I recommend making a formal review after three months and every six months thereafter for the first two years of an employee's tenure. Try to answer the following questions:

- Do I have any second thoughts about this employee?
- Does the employee have any second thoughts about his or her decision to accept the job?
- Would I rehire the employee at this time?
- If the same job were offered to this employee now, would he or she accept it?

CHAPTER 10

Work Environment Problems

WHILE employees' perceptions of the work environment vary, there is a certain type of work climate that is unhealthy for many employees and that may even force them out of the organization.

In follow-up interviews, many former employees cite dissatisfaction with the work environment as a major reason for leaving. For example:

"They just didn't care about people. No one was interested in my needs, aspirations, or problems. I felt like an interchangeable part. If I malfunctioned, no attempt would be made to repair or salvage me. I would just be replaced with someone else."

"That company was an ulcer factory. The work demands were overwhelming. Every day was filled with unrelenting deadlines and crises."

"When I first started at the company, I was naive enough to believe that if I worked hard and performed well, I would succeed. It was disillusioning to discover that the only thing that really mattered was aligning yourself with the political factions that were in power so you could become eligible for a sinecure."

When employees talk about the work environment in their former company, their comments are usually loaded with emotion. They feel hurt and bitter, and claim there are many others like them who are still with the company.

From work climate surveys at client organizations and follow-up interviews with former employees, I have developed a checklist of "Ways of Creating an Unhealthy Work Environment." (See Figure 15.) Let's take a close look at it and review the common practices that spoil a work environment. These can be categorized under five headings: values, relationships, inequities, trespasses, and uncertainties.

VALUES

The values of an organization are reflected in the behavior of its managers. Norms are established, and it is extremely uncomfortable for anyone who dares to depart from those norms.

A common company value that can lead to turnover is "Don't pamper employees. Give them only what you must." For example, maintain the compensation level at the industry average or slightly below average. Or train employees to meet specific needs, not for general development.

Another destructive value is "Focus your attention on

Figure 15. Creating an unhealthy work environment.

Values	☐ Give *only* what you must. ☐ Value groups; ignore individuals. ☐ Don't trust employees.
Relationships	☐ Encourage adversary relationships. ☐ Introduce sudden change. ☐ Strain relationships.
Inequities	☐ Give unequal rewards and stakes. ☐ Assign unequal quantity and quality of work. ☐ Provide unequal opportunities.
Trespasses	☐ Interfere with home life. ☐ Give overlapping assignments. ☐ Interfere with work responsibility.
Uncertainties	☐ Don't keep employees well informed. ☐ Issue inconsistent policies and procedures and change them regularly. ☐ Don't let employees know how they stand.

the work group, not on individuals." Managers who support this philosophy sacrifice individual needs for "the good of the group." While this may appear to be a reasonable approach, in practice it leads to unnecessary abuses. For example, in an engineering group it was a common practice for members to rotate as project team leaders. A new departmental manager changed the system for "the good of the group." He claimed that the department looked bad because of poor leadership in some of its projects. Therefore, he appointed several people as permanent project leaders, denying the opportunity to others in the group. As a result, within three months two highly experienced, outstanding performers left; within six months, two more left the group.

Another value that can create an unhealthy work climate is "Don't trust subordinates. If you don't watch them carefully, they will take advantage of you." Managers who espouse this view create a closed work environment, characterized by suspicion, coldness, and guardedness. Employees feel that they are continually under surveillance and become overly concerned about what they say or do.

RELATIONSHIPS

A work environment that encourages adversary relationships drives away employees. In the name of competitiveness, managers pit one employee against another. Coopcrativeness is discouraged. Adversaries are less interested in meeting corporate objectives and getting the job done than they are in achieving their own objectives. They focus on "What will make me look good?" and "How can I make the other person look bad so I can look better?"

Sometimes a work environment becomes inhospitable because of a change in relationships. Usually the catalyst is the replacement of top management. Favored employees suddenly find themselves in disfavor. For example, one company acquired a new top management as a result of a merger. The new leaders brought with them an entourage, forming an ingroup with very limited membership. Subsequently, there was a large number of terminations and resignations.

When employees are under extreme pressure, relationships are strained, and the work environment can become inhospitable. Deadlines, bottlenecks, crises, budget shortfalls, sales downtrends, competitive threats—all create pressures that disrupt smooth working relationships. For example, when an account group at an advertising agency began to face complaints from a major client, the work environment deteriorated. Previously, the members of the account group had worked well together. But as the client's complaints grew more serious, members of the group attempted to avoid responsibility for the problem. Their performance was plummeted as they blamed each other for what was happening.

INEQUITIES

Whenever employees believe that they are not getting a fair share of rewards, status, workload, or opportunities, the work environment becomes inhospitable. Even if managers are completely committed to "equal treatment" for all subordinates, at times some subordinates will feel that managers are unfair.

Employees are particularly sensitive to inequities in the distribution of rewards and status. While many employees want more than they deserve, they know when fellow employees are outperforming them and therefore deserve greater rewards and status. However, when they feel that I-am-just-as-good-as fellow employees are receiving greater rewards and status, their positive feelings about the work environment will be dispelled rapidly. For example, in one data processing organization, a well-liked but marginal performer was named branch manager. Subsequently, there was a rash of resignations as employees reacted to what they considered an "act of unfairness."

Often, the distribution of the workload—in quantity and quality—can become a source of perceived inequities. Employees are willing to shoulder their fair share of the work, and of "grunt" assignments. But whenever they feel they are being overloaded, particularly with assignments that are routine and undesirable, they become unhappy with the work environment. For example, in the clinical laboratory of a leading hospital, the night shift believed that the day shift was deliberately dumping part of its workload on them. In addition, the day shift tended to leave work areas dirty, so that the night shift was burdened with cleanup. Because of this perceived inequity, turnover in the night shift was nearly double that in the day shift.

Concern about unequal advancement opportunities can also lead to dissatisfaction. Employees may feel that supervisors favor certain co-workers for personal reasons and give them preferential treatment. Or they may believe that "people from our department" don't get a chance to move up.

Related to concern about unequal opportunity is the feeling of being "held back" in a routine job that does not offer the employee a sense of achievement or an opportunity to learn new skills. Employees recognize that if they can't demonstrate their abilities in significant projects, they hurt their chances of being considered for promotion. And if they don't continually develop their abilities, they will become "stale" and less valuable to their own company and to other organizations.

When employees have limited opportunities for learning and development, concern with "lack of career advancement" intensifies and may lead to turnover. For example, an engineer who regularly handles the same kinds of projects with no change in routine is much more apt to consider leaving a job than a colleague who periodically receives special assignments. Both may not have any opportunity for career advancement, but one has an opportunity to achieve, learn, and develop.

TRESPASSES

An invasion of employees' territorial rights can create an unhealthy work environment. Employees have a strong sense of what belongs to them and resent any unlawful entries into their territory.

One territory that is particularly well protected is the home. When job responsibilities spill over into home life and free time, employees become extremely concerned.

For example, in one organization it was common practice to hold late staff meetings and to force employees to work on Saturday. Some employees resented this intrusion and eventually left their jobs because of it.

Trespassing ofter occurs on employees' job territory as well. In distributing work, managers give subordinates overlapping assignments. This leads to considerable friction, and eventually to turnover. For example, in one company organized along product lines, product managers had to compete with one another for funds. The competition created a hostile work environment which proved to be insupportable for some of the managers.

Another type of invasion involves interference with work responsibility. Employees regard some of their work responsibilities as their own. They expect to satisfy these responsibilities autonomously, being accountable only for results. They are very protective of their freedom of action in obtaining those results. If immediate supervision or higher management "sticks its fingers in the pie," employees will grow resentful and may ultimately leave the company.

UNCERTAINTIES

When a company keeps employees guessing about what's going to happen next, the work environment becomes unhealthy. Most employees feel insecure in an environment that is not somewhat predictable.

Employees who feel that they are being kept in the dark will attempt to fill in the gaps with rumors and gossip. The grapevine is kept busy, usually with misinformation that alarms employees and fans dissatisfaction. For example, the new administrators of a hospital were closed-mouthed. During their first few months in office they conducted a study of operations, and everyone in the hospital expected changes. The waiting for the "ax to fall" proved to be too much for some employees, particularly those who were able to find new jobs quickly.

Organizations that issue inconsistent policies and procedures and then continually change them also create an unhealthy work environment. Most employees want to "play by the rules" and are upset when they don't know what the rules are. For example, the sales manager of a large pharmaceuticals company, in response to pressures from above, issued five different policies and procedures on territorial coverage during a two-year period. Within that time there was a marked increase in turnover.

One area in which it is particularly important to keep employees well informed is performance appraisal. Employees want to know where they stand. They have very little tolerance of uncertainty. For example, an increase in turnover in one organization was directly associated with the installation of a new performance appraisal program based on management by objectives. Neither the employees nor the managers understood the MBO system well. As a result, everyone was uncertain about performance criteria. It took about a year for the employees and managers to feel comfortable with the system, and for turnover to subside.

COMMONSENSE ACTIONS

1. Every manager should install an early-warning system to detect employee concern with changed relationships, inequities, trespasses, and uncertainties. Two techniques that I have found especially helpful are the *slip session* and the *frustration box*. In a slip session, the manager assembles his or her staff in order to identify problems in the work environment. Staff members are asked to take several pieces of paper and tear them into parts, so that each has at least twelve slips. They they are instructed to identify one problem on each slip of paper. The slips are collected and sorted. The problems are discussed, starting with those mentioned most frequently.

The frustration box, like the slip session, encourages employees to identify problems anonymously. Whenever employees feel concerned about a problem in the work environment, they go over to the frustration box, fill out a 3″ × 5″ card, and deposit it in the box. (See Figure 16.)

2. It is helpful for managers to conduct a *survey of values* regularly. At least once a year, ask your subordinates to complete the following sentences:

The company is interested in . . .

The company isn't interested in . . .

My manager is interested in . . .

My manager isn't interested in . . .

To help stimulate their thinking, provide them with the following list of possible answers:

. . . creating more varied and challenging jobs.

. . . providing job security and reasonable financial rewards.

. . . helping to train and develop employees.

. . . reducing stress on employees.

. . . encouraging cooperation.

. . . providing reasonable working hours.

. . . providing good working conditions.

3. Whenever an official communication is sent to staff members announcing changes that affect them, the man-

Figure 16. Frustration box card.

Date _____

What's bothering you?

What brought about the problem?

What do you feel should be done?

ager should provide a mechanism for *immediate* feedback. For example, you might send employees a colored sheet of paper with the following questions:

How will the proposed change affect you?

How do you feel about the proposed change?

4. Meet with each employee at least once every quarter to discuss performance. To make these short appraisal sessions more meaningful, have the employee come prepared with answers to the following self-appraisal questions:

What areas of your work are going well?

What areas of your work are not going well?

In what areas of your job do you feel you need to improve your skills?

What kind of help do you need from your manager or others in the organization?

5. Too much or too little change may precipitate feelings of dissatisfaction. If your subordinates report negative feelings in completing the survey of values, accept the feelings as legitimate. Then try to help employees confront their feelings. For example:

SUPERVISOR   From your responses to the survey, it appears that this last year has been upsetting to you.

SUBORDINATE   It sure has been! My boss, and closest friend in the company, was fired. And you took over his job and completely changed my work assignment.

SUPERVISOR   I can appreciate how you feel. If I were you, I might feel the same way. But does it help you to be so upset?

SUBORDINATE   What do you mean, "Does it help me?" I don't like being upset. And I'm certainly not responsible for what's happened to me this year.

SUPERVISOR   No, you're not responsible for what has happened. But you're responsible for what happens next.

SUBORDINATE   What do you mean?

SUPERVISOR   Well, you can prolong the period that you're upset and can choose to feel even worse. Or you can do something about getting rid of those feelings.

SUBORDINATE   What can I do?

SUPERVISOR To start with, you can first decide to stop feeling bad. Those feelings don't help you; in fact, they hurt you. Once you do that, we can discuss our relationship, and your work assignment, and see if we can work out a mutually satisfying arrangement. Perhaps I can give you more freedom of action. Or I may be able to assign work projects more to your liking and eliminate some of the routine assignments.

Hopefully, as the discussion develops, the subordinate will try to resolve his negative feelings, and emerge with a strengthened relationship with the supervisor and better feelings about his work assignment.

CHAPTER 11

Work Assignment Problems

MANY people accept jobs that are wrong for them. They step blindly into work assignments that in a short time they won't want, urged on by hiring managers who care little about their needs. Hiring managers are intent on finding out whether potential employees have the ability to perform a job, while candidates for employment are primarily interested in getting a job—even one they know little about. The hiring manager's strong desire to "fill a vacancy" and the candidate's strong desire to "land a job" interfere with a real matching of candidate and job.

Naturally, hiring managers don't create a mismatch deliberately. Nevertheless, their actions often lead to placing a candidate in an unsuitable work assignment. When I pointed out this fact to a hiring manager, he quickly understood what I was talking about:

> "I guess I have nobody to blame but myself. I was so intent on recruiting a subordinate I could show off that I forgot about the job specifications. I insisted on the candidate who was in the top 5 percent of the class and who scored top grades in the battery of tests our company administered. I forgot I was hiring for a job that didn't give an employee much opportunity to show initiative and that was not regarded as a steppingstone to better positions.

> "To make matters worse, the candidate I eventually hired had some reservations about the job. Even though I presented a very positive picture, emphasizing the good parts of the job, he was concerned about the scope of the job as outlined in the job description. However, I convinced him otherwise."

This hiring manager made two major selection errors: he didn't pay sufficient attention to the job specification, and he didn't present both sides of the job to the prospective candidate. Unfortunately, similar mistakes are repeated daily by many managers. Either they don't take the trouble to prepare a thorough job specification or they ignore the specification they prepared. And then, once impressed with a candidate's credentials, they make sure that the candidate "won't get away" by overselling the company and the job.

On the other hand, the job seeker is also responsible for the mismatch. Many eager candidates are willing to accept a job that is not in their best interests. They focus only on "getting ahead" and "making more money." These two short-term objectives overshadow more important long-term personal objectives. Only later do the candidates realize their mistake. As one young woman told me during a follow-up interview:

"I felt that I was playing catchup. I returned to the workforce after having stayed at home for nearly five years raising a family. I liked my job in the company, but when a management search firm approached me and described a job at a higher level that paid nearly 20 percent more, I found it hard to think about anything else. I asked very few questions about the job or the new company. Instead, I was determined to get that position.

"Well, I was successful in getting the job. I just wish I hadn't been so convincing. It's been only four months since I left the other company, but I know I've made a mistake. The new job is a complete departure from anything I've done in the past. I don't like the work, and I don't feel I have a real aptitude for it. Besides, I think it's a blind alley."

Job seekers are notoriously inept at *reverse* interviewing. They don't know how to ask the right questions to become better informed about the new job. They are reluctant to say anything that might make them appear to be less than enthusiastic about the job opening.

Besides not learning about the new job, they fail to consider their own values and needs and the role they play in a job match. Here are three case histories of mismatches that could have been avoided if the job seekers had known themselves better:

Sharon had extraordinary talent in computer programming. As colleagues described her, "She and the computer make music." She loved to tackle complex programming assignments. She applied her full energy and concentration to them, working for long hours at her desk until she created a workable program.

She never considered changing jobs until one of the other programmers accepted a position as administrative head of the computer department in another company. Thereafter, she convinced herself that she should be more career-minded and concerned with advancement. Within a year she found another position, at a managerial level—only to learn, too late, that she preferred programming to management.

Ernie left his position as top salesman in a company to assume the management of his father-in-law's retail business. Ernie was accustomed to, and enjoyed, dealing with top-level managers in sales situations rather than dealing directly with the public. In addition, he had always disliked even the minimal paperwork associated with his sales job, and now he hated the heavy paperwork required of him as manager of a retail business.

Ernie achieved the high income level his father-in-law had promised, only to find that money wasn't as important to him as he had thought. He had made an adequate income before, doing work that suited him naturally. In his new capacity, the work assignment was a force-fit.

Rose was a satisfied teacher who had worked in the same school system for 10 years. When she was divorced, her financial needs increased, so she sought employment in industry.

Because she had taught a foreign language, she was able to get a substantial position in the international department of a major corporation. It offered her money, status, and varied work assignments. What it didn't give her, and what she sorely missed, was the sense of fulfillment she had derived from teaching. She realized that she had paid a heavy price for the luxuries she could now afford for her family.

STARTING OFF ON THE WRONG FOOT

Even when new employees are placed in work assignments which they are capable of doing and ordinarily would be content with, the orientation period may turn them off. It may be abbreviated or prolonged. It may be insufficiently demanding or overdemanding. Any number of orientation errors can get employees started on the wrong foot.

Length of Orientation

The length of the orientation period should be determined by the complexity of the job and the ability of the new employee to master requisite skills. Often, the orientation program is not well thought out and the employee is rushed through it. The manager may have insufficient time to spend with the new employee, or may simply be unwilling to take the time. Perhaps the manager is anxious to unload duties on the new employee that he had to temporarily assume while the job was vacant. Managers feel that if they "tell" employees what to do, they have satisfied their responsibility. However, they leave employees with a lot of unanswered questions. The uninformed employees step into uncomfortable situations that can create irreversible bad feelings.

On the other hand, if the orientation period is prolonged, employees get the feeling that they will never assume their rightful responsibilities. Instead, the manager doles out assignments one at a time. He is unwilling to relinquish them because he enjoys doing them himself or is afraid to delegate. As a result, new employees receive routine, nonstimulating assignments and rarely get an opportunity to use their initiative or develop their skills. Often, by the time these employees start to assume more responsibility, they have already become disenchanted with the job and the organization. Also, they may be anxious to "catch up" and assume greater responsibility at an accelerated rate. So, whatever expansion of the work assignment has already taken place, it is viewed as "too late and not enough."

Demands of Orientation

Depending on the demands made during orientation, an employee may get the impression that a work assignment is one that "I can do with my eyes closed" or one that is "more than I can handle." If the orientation is insufficiently demanding, the employee may feel that the job duties are too light. The training may be too basic. The workload may be insufficient. The initial performance expectations may be too low—the employee may be able to meet the standards with no effort at all. As a result of this initial "soft" treatment, the employee may learn to coast on the job, developing a work pattern that will eventually lead to problems.

Just as damaging is an overly demanding orientation. The training may be too intense and comprehensive. The initial workload may be overwhelming. And the standards and expectations for the new employee may be unrealistically high.

Whether the orientation is underdemanding or overdemanding, the employee forms first impressions that are hard to erase. If new employees develop bad feelings from the start, they may still harbor these feelings when conditions change.

Protectiveness During Orientation

Managers vary greatly in their willingness to protect new employees from "hard knocks." Some managers are overly protective. They carefully screen assignments and contacts, minimizing risks for new employees. When disagreements arise, they champion new employees, fighting their battles and solving their problems. Naturally, in this kind of protective environment, employees can become overly dependent. And complications arise when the employees become resentful of being dependent or when their managers decide that orientation is over and start to expect more independence.

In contrast to the overly protective manager is the manager who throws new employees to the wolves. Such a manager allows employees to tackle problems they are not ready to handle or to do battle with opponents who completely outclass them. The battering that employees receive during this period can be permanently damaging.

Their abilities may become suspect because of costly mistakes they have made. And they may accumulate detractors and enemies as a result of their missteps.

Employee Outgrows Job

Employees may be right for the job when they are hired, but as they grow personally they may outgrow the job—or think they've outgrown it.

Often, postgraduate education will make employees feel they have outgrown their jobs. For example, several years ago I participated in career counseling interviews with part-time MBA students at the Fairleigh Dickinson Graduate School of Business. As they neared graduation, the students became much more aware of the need to expand their responsibilities at work and to use their newly acquired skills. After graduation, a sizable number of them became frustrated at work and sought new employment.

Sometimes managers allow employees to temporarily expand their responsibilities, giving them a taste of more challenging and rewarding work. For example, an employee may take part in a special task force or may fill in while a manager is occupied in a special assignment. Or, as part of a management development program, the employee may be given a special short-term assignment. Whatever the reasons for the short-term expansion of responsibilities, employees enjoy the change in work assignment and learn that they are capable of performing at a higher level. Often, when they return to their original assignment, they find it very difficult to be as satisfied as they had been previously.

Even when employees are not exposed to a temporary step-up in responsibility, they may come to feel they have outgrown their jobs. Perhaps friends or colleagues encourage them to seek extra responsibility. Or perhaps they see colleagues being given extra responsibility and believe they deserve it too. Or they may feel envious of colleagues in comparable positions who have much greater freedom of action.

Job Outgrows Employee

The growth of an employee may not keep pace with the growth of responsibility in the job. This is particularly true of high-technology jobs that demand a regular renewal of skills. In these situations, past experience becomes a liability rather than an asset. Often newer, more recently trained employees are more capable of doing the job than older employees whose skills have become outdated.

Restructuring of the organization can also lead to expansion of job responsibilities beyond the capability of the jobholder. The restructuring may create a heavier workload or call for a speedup in work pace that the jobholder can't satisfy.

Sometimes, particularly among employees who have been in the same job five or more years, a loss of interest in the job or a preoccupation with off-the-job activities may prevent employees from performing satisfactorily. The employees find that they are no longer able to "stay on top of the job."

THE IMPACT OF CHANGE—OR LACK OF IT

In most companies, work assignments don't stay the same. Economic fluctuations, reorganizations, shifts in key people, and changes in the company's rate of growth affect the workload and the demands made on employees. Some employees are able to adapt to change with no difficulty, while others view any change in their work assignment as threatening and fear that they will no longer be able to handle the job.

Lack of change over prolonged periods can also create problems. In fact, the main complaint of employees who have been in the same job for five or more years—the "nonpromotables"—is the daily drudgery of an unchanging job. They become dissatisfied with doing the same things day after day.

Thus, even though an employee may be initially placed

in the right work assignment, it may develop into the wrong work assignment. And people in the wrong work assignment become increasingly dissatisfied. Eventually, they may seek relief by leaving the organization.

COMMONSENSE ACTIONS

1. To avoid placing employees in inappropriate work assignments, try to give every prospective candidate a thorough job preview. Ideally, the candidate should be given an opportunity to meet future co-workers and to see the kinds of duties that the job entails. If such a preview is not feasible, you should give the applicant a broad and fair perspective of the job, paying particular attention to things that may be important from the applicant's point of view.

2. To facilitate matching employees with job assignments, you may find it helpful to have applicants write a work autobiography, describing their work experience and the kinds of activities they enjoyed doing and did well. If possible, offer applicants a copy of the book *What Color Is Your Parachute: A Practical Manual for Job-Hunters and Career-Changers.** This manual explains how to write a work autobiography and gives readers many insights into work activities that are appropriate for them.

3. Once you hire a candidate for a job, take the time and effort to make certain that the employee receives a thorough orientation. If you decide to delegate the responsibility for orientation to one of your subordinates, plan to conduct 30-, 60-, and 90-day follow-up interviews. During these interviews, determine how well the new employee understands the job and the organization. In particular, probe for any developing problems, either in the job itself or in relationships with people in the organization.

4. Since changes in work assignment can affect employ-

---

*Richard N. Bolles, *What Color Is Your Parachute? A Practical Manual for Job-Hunters and Career-Changers*, 5th rev. ed. (Berkeley, CA: Ten Speed Press, 1978).

Figure 17. Survey of change.

1. In the last year, has your work assignment changed? In what ways (new activities, new relationships, new skill requirements, and so on)?

2. Have your feelings about your work assignment changed? Better? Worse? Why?

3. How much has your job changed over the last *three* years? What were the changes? Good or bad?

ees' feelings about their jobs, you might plan to conduct a *survey of change* annually, or whenever dramatic organizationwide changes occur. The simple survey shown in Figure 17 is useful for this purpose.

CHAPTER 12

Pay and Benefits Problems

THERE is no question that pay rates can influence turn-over, particularly in inflationary times. People legitimately leave companies for "more money." And people who are paid exceptionally well are probably less likely to leave an organization than people who are not paid well.

However, managers generally overestimate the significance of pay. There is a sizable literature that questions the impact of high pay on reducing turnover, and researchers have demonstrated that pay is less important to some groups of employees than to others.

Perhaps the reason managers overestimate the significance of pay is that many employees claim they are leaving the organization for "more money." But often the pay complaints are a coverup for other concerns and problems. For example, in a follow-up study of 50 voluntary leavers who cited inadequate pay as their primary reason for leaving, I found that only 12 of these employees—24 percent— had legitimate pay complaints. And in no case did the absolute compensation gain in the next job exceed 20 percent.

From company to company, the differences in absolute amount of pay (salary, bonus, and benefits) for comparable jobs is relatively low. Yet employees in one organization may be quite dissatisfied with the compensation program, while employees in comparable jobs in other organizations, making similar wages, may be much more satisfied. Obviously, the way the compensation program is administered can contribute to employees' satisfaction.

KEY PAY POLICY ISSUES

Employee satisfaction or dissatisfaction often depends on the organization's pay policy. Let's examine ten key pay policy issues and how they are confronted by employees.

ISSUE	CONFRONTATION
Equitability	"He's making more money for the same job."
Personal needs	"I've got to get more money."
Automatic/standard increases	"It doesn't pay to do a good job."
Cost-of-living increases	"Other companies are giving cost-of-living increases."
Minimums and maximums	"Is that the most I can make?"
Spread	"Is she that much better?"
Market value	"Other companies pay more."

ISSUE	CONFRONTATION
Government guidelines	"You're hiding behind government pay guidelines."
Incentives	"I would prefer to be paid for time."
Benefits	"Not the same as pay."

Equitability

Although many organizations are secretive about salary levels, employees have a way of finding out how much co-workers are making. They "keep score," continually comparing wages for comparable work assignments.

When a red-faced employee confronts a supervisor and says, "Joe is making more money than I am for the same job," he is concerned about equitability. Probably, the employee has mentally compared his own skills, responsibilities, performance, and effort with those of the co-worker and concluded that he is "as good as" or "better than" the co-worker. Usually, such comparisons are based on filtered information and are distorted by personal bias. Most of the time we look better to ourselves than to others, especially since we tend to rationalize our shortcomings.

Personal Needs

The employee who tells her manager, "I've got to get more money," probably accurately recognizes her needs. Perhaps she has had some unusual expenses or has mismanaged her finances. But does her financial need justify a salary increase?

Some employees feel the only way to respond to financial pressures is to get another job that pays more. However, they don't consider the long-term consequences of changing jobs and allowing a short-term financial problem to compromise their careers.

Often, in changing jobs employees don't even satisfy their short-term financial problems. The extra salary they receive from another organization is usually insufficient to relieve extraordinary financial problems. For example, one engineer I know overextended himself financially. In a relatively short period of time, he purchased a new home, automobile, and boat—all with minimum downpayments and heavy credit charges. Pressed to keep up with his bills, he left a job that he "really liked" to join an organization that he described as being unconcerned about employees as people and making unreasonable demands on them. The extra 20 percent he received in salary made little difference in his ability to pay his bills. Eventually, he had to sell the boat, trade in his new car for an older, smaller model, and move into an apartment. The only thing he managed to keep was a job he disliked, in a company that wasn't concerned about him.

Automatic/Standard Salary Increases

Although most organizations claim to give *merit* salary increases, in effect the salary increases are automatic and standard. Employees know that unless they have fouled up badly in the past year, they will get a salary increase, and that the increase will be somewhere between 5 and 10 percent. Such an automatic increase policy may lead employees to conlude, "It doesn't pay to do a good job."

Often, managers are responsible for deemphasizing *merit* in salary administration. They're fearful of changing the salary distribution pattern, giving more money to some employees and less to others. One manager candidly expressed her concern when she said:

"I have good relationships with all the people who work for me. I know they all try to do a good job. I feel that if I did not encourage the low performers and bypassed their salary increases, they would only perform worse. On the other hand, if I took the money gained by not giving some employees salary increases and gave it to the high performers, they would not perform any better.

Instead, everybody gets a salary increase: the low performers receive somewhat less, and the high performers receive somewhat more."

Unfortunately, this type of thinking can lead to employee dissatisfaction with pay policy. And in the process the organization may lose the employees it least wants to lose—the high performers.

Cost-of-Living Increases

As prices soar and inflation makes it harder for people to maintain their standard of living, employees expect the company to do something about it. When a company in the area, or in the industry, gives its employees a cost-of-living salary adjustment, employees in other companies want one too.

This issue will probably become more serious in the next few years as the rate of inflation moves upward. Unquestionably, inflation affects us all, but not equally. And the impact of this issue on turnover is related to whether employees believe the organization intends to maintain a competitive pay policy.

Minimums and Maximums

Job evaluation is a common practice in many organizations. The end result of job evaluation is to establish minimum and maximum salary ranges for each job. However, employees often disagree with the minimums and maximums that are established and feel that they are "locked in" by them. This leads to a common complaint: "Is that the most I can make?"

The salary range is viewed as having chiseled-in-stone limits. Employees falsely believe that these limits represent a barrier to their personal financial growth, rather than representing an evaluation of the market value of their job at the current time. If the job grows in responsibility, the salary limits should change. And by the time an employee reaches the maximum, he or she may be ready for a promotion, or the job may have increased in market value.

Spread

The dollar differential between the salary levels of high performers and low performers is of particular concern to employees. High performers expect there to be a reasonable spread between their salary level and that of low performers. On the other hand, low performers who feel they are expending as much effort as high performers resent an excessively large spread. They complain, "I know Joe's a high performer, but is he that much better than I am?"

"Spread" becomes an increasingly urgent issue as compensation programs continue to favor high performers. Year by year, the spread between the salaries of high performers and low performers keeps widening.

Market Value

As employees master jobs, adding and developing skills, they increase their market value. Often, this change in market value is ignored by their employer. The only way employees can call attention to it is by checking out their market value and alerting management to what they have learned in the job market: "Other companies are paying more for the same job."

Of course, by the time employees bring their market value to the attention of supervisors, they may have already decided to leave the organization. And supervisors who are so confronted may feel that they are being "backed to the wall" and may refuse to negotiate salary.

Government Guidelines

The government's 7 percent pay guideline is viewed by some organizations as a way to keep the cost of salary increases down. But rather than trying to keep the total payroll below 7 percent, balancing out increases above and below that percentage, many managers arbitrarily limit all salary increases to 7 percent. This practice leads to considerable dissatisfaction, and a prevailing feeling among employees that the organization is "hiding behind the government's pay guidelines."

Recently, I conducted an attitude survey for a company and learned that most of its employees believed that management was "delighted" with the 7 percent pay guideline and that the company adhered to it more rigorously than did other organizations. The only employees who did not share this attitude were those in units whose managers had explained the guideline and administered it intelligently.

Incentives

Numerous research studies have demonstrated that employees can be motivated to increase their output with incentive pay. But incentive programs are beset with problems, as anybody who has ever managed a sales force knows. Certainly, incentive plans raise questions about equitability, spread, and market value. In addition, employees quickly become accustomed to a level of income that includes a certain portion of incentive earnings. Should that level drop in subsequent years, employees will feel they have received a salary cut. Naturally, considerable dissatisfaction can result.

For example, one organization introduced an exclusive product that quickly captured a giant share of the market. The company's sales people enjoyed the benefits of this product introduction, reaping windfall incentive earnings. Eventually, when the growth of the product stabilized, the amount of incentive pay declined, and the turnover rate increased as dissatisfied employees complained about "salary reduction."

Benefits

Benefits are not uniformly attractive to all employees. Certainly, a security-conscious older employee will be interested in retirement benefits. And an employee facing.

high medical costs will be interested in the medical benefits package. However, as many employees have told me in the past, "Benefits are not the same as pay."

Some organizations emphasize benefits at the expense of salary. Employees who are not concerned with benefits may be attracted by other organizations that offer lower benefits and higher salary.

COMMONSENSE ACTIONS

While most managers realize that pay issues are related to turnover, they feel that pay policy is determined at the corporate level and that they have no control over it. However, there are many commonsense actions that managers can and should take.

1. Explore each pay complaint thoroughly to make sure that you are really dealing with a money issue. Remember, pay complaints are often a coverup for other concerns and problems.

2. In any discussion about pay complaints, make certain that the employee understands your organization's pay policy and knows that its objective is to provide a "fair day's work for a fair day's pay." Explain how job evaluation ensures equity and places a competitive price tag on a job: it defines the job and doesn't set limits on the person's financial growth.

3. Regularly reevaluate the market value of employees who report to you. If your organization participates in an annual salary survey, use the information in making your assessment. If not, you can gather information on competitive salaries from colleagues at other organizations, from employment search organizations, and from job applicants.

4. Keep track of the cost-of-living changes in geographical areas of interest to you and compare them with national cost-of-living changes. For example, if you supervise people in a branch office in a part of the country that is hard hit by cost-of-living changes, you may want to recommend a salary adjustment, particularly if other organizations in the area have a higher pay scale.

5. Individualize the timing of pay increases. If possible, award merit increases immediately after a period of outstanding performance. In this way employees will recognize that merit increases are performance-related rather than time-related.

6. Base percentage increases on salary range midpoints rather than on actual salaries. This practice prevents the spread between the salaries of high performers and low performers from becoming too wide. Suppose, for example, that the salary range for a given job is $1,000 to $2,000 per month and that the average low performer is currently earning $1,000 per month and the average high performer $1,500. If both are awarded 7 percent increases based on current salary, the low performer will get an increase of only $70 per month while the high performer will get an increase of $105. However, if the 7 percent increase is based on the midpoint of the salary range, or $1,500, both the low performer and the high performer will receive a salary increase of $105 per month.

7. If your company adheres to government pay guidelines, distribute salary increases over fewer people. Rather than giving out token salary increases, award only merit increases. Thus low performers should be bypassed so that high performers can get salary increases above 7 percent. Naturally, low performers will be dissatisfied and you will have to counsel them, explaining what they will have to do to get a merit increase in the future.

8. Don't try to buy employee satisfaction. It's your responsibility to make certain that employees are not overpaid and that salary administration is equitable. Only poor managers overpay employees. Overpayment won't guarantee the retention of high performers in the face of strong dissatisfaction with other aspects of the work environment.

CHAPTER 13

Promotion Problems

WHENEVER the number of employees ready for promotion and the number of available openings are out of balance, turnover increases. In the interest of "getting ahead," employees must move from one organization to another. However, employees have to observe social norms which dictate the frequency and total number of "permissible" job changes; otherwise, they risk being labeled job hoppers.

The imbalance is magnified by inaccurate employee perceptions of their "readiness" for promotion. An employee may be:

Ready and qualified.
Ready but not qualified.

Not ready but qualified.
Not ready and not qualified.

Let's examine the possible problems associated with each of these four conditions.

Ready and Qualified

If employees believe they are ready for promotion, and are in fact qualified for promotion, they will be justifiably anxious to change jobs. The longer they remain in a state of readiness without receiving advancement, the more likely they are to become discontent. This problem is particularly prevalent in mature organizations whose growth has slowed and in organizations in which advanced positions are held by long-term, older employees who have "settled into" their jobs.

Ready but Not Qualified

Perhaps because of self-deception or a misunderstanding of the requirements for the next career step, some employees believe that they are ready for advancement when they are not qualified. When these employees are passed by for promotion, they can't understand it, because they are blind to the fact that they are not qualified.

Not Ready but Qualified

Employees who are psychologically unprepared for promotion yet fully qualified pose a problem only if they suddenly realize they are qualified and blame the organization for not having advanced them. Many employees in this category are solid "company" people who rely on the organization to take care of them. Since they exert no pressure for advancement, other, more ambitious employees are given opportunities that should have been theirs.

Not Ready and Not Qualified

Employees who are neither ready nor qualified are the least likely to pose promotion problems. Both trainees and nonpromotables may fit into this category. Until trainees gain enough skills to feel that they are qualified for promotion, they are usually content to stay in the same job. Nonpromotables may also be content to stay in their jobs if they don't want promotion and realize that they are not qualified for the next career step.

However, trainees sometimes believe that they have "learned the job" even though their managers disagree. And nonpromotables, because of social pressures from family members or co-workers, may be prodded into seeking a promotion which they really don't want and for which they do not feel qualified.

Short Chain of Progression

The imbalance between promotional opportunities and the number of available, qualified employees is particularly marked in certain specialties where the chain of progression is very short. For example, engineers may find that they run out of advancement opportunities much faster than colleagues in other functional areas. Similarly, computer programmers may face a short chain of progression.

Contributing to the imbalance is an unequal distribution of openings within the organization. A company's growth may be reflected in the demand for expansion only in specific operations within the company, specific geographic areas, or specific job titles. Thus the organization may have to search for outsiders to fill jobs which it is unable to offer its own employees.

As the imbalance grows, an increasing number of employees feel they are underutilized and are being held back.

Questioning Criteria for Qualification

The issue of qualification can become very heated if performance appraisal is highly subjective and the criteria for promotion are poorly defined. For example, some managers advance employees they like and work well with, rather than matching an employee's qualifications with the requirements of the higher-level job. As a result, politically adept employees, sponsored by influentials, may move ahead faster than more qualified co-workers who are not being sponsored.

High visibility and being in the "right place at the right time" can also win promotion for employees. More qualified employees who perform outstandingly are overlooked, because they are never brought to the attention of the right people.

"Costs" of Promotion

After the initial positive effects of a promotion wear off, employees may find that they encounter problems. A high performer in one kind of job may discover that he doesn't like and has difficulty performing the newer job. Perhaps he was an outstanding individual performer but lacks the aptitude to manage others. He may have had greater freedom of action and more autonomy in the lower-level job. It's even possible that his total compensation package, including incentive pay, was higher in his former job.

Sometimes a valuable employee is thrust into a new job prematurely. The subsequent problems she has in performing the job may weaken her self-confidence and lower her standing in the eyes of colleagues. As a result, she may be forced out of the organization or may leave voluntarily to get a fresh start.

Many promoted employees feel that the price they pay for promotion is too great. There may be much greater risk associated with the higher-level job and much greater stress. For modest financial gains, employees who had been content in lower-level jobs may find themselves feeling insecure and harassed. Another cost of promotion is the time employees must spend learning the new job. That time is usually taken away from their personal lives.

Employees may incur other "costs" as well. They may not like their new co-workers. They may have to travel more. They may have to shoulder a heavier workload.

They may inherit a whole new set of problems. Or a "whole lot of little things" may make them feel the benefits of the new job are not worth the costs.

Onlookers to Promotion

Promotions not only affect the employees directly involved—those considered for promotion and those actually promoted—they also affect interested onlookers in the company. Employees judge the organization on the fairness of its promotions. If an older employee is passed by for promotion, then all older employees may feel that they are dead-ended. If a minority employee fails to win a promotion, other minorities in the organization may feel that their chances for promotion are diminished. When unqualified employees are promoted, more qualified employees may believe, rightly or wrongly, that they are in disfavor and would probably be better off in another organization.

In studying individual promotions in one company, I discovered that virtually all of them had a significant impact on other people, and some of them had extraordinary impact:

- Employees left the organization because others were promoted to jobs they wanted.
- Multiple resignations followed the appointment of an unqualified employee.
- A number of newly appointed managers resigned or were terminated within the first year.
- Newly appointed managers "cleaned house" shortly after they took over.

Breaking the News to Bypassed Employees

Anyone who has been passed by for promotion naturally feels disappointed. Managers can make the situation better or worse, depending on how sensitive they are in "breaking the news." Often, the only thing a subordinate gets from his or her manager is a brief announcement that someone else was promoted and a vague explanation:

"A more qualified employee was appointed."
"You didn't have the right kind of experience."
"The person who got the promotion has been with the company a longer time."

Sometimes, too, the employee gets no explanation at all. Listen to the complaints of these disgrunted employees:

"I didn't know that somebody else had gotten the promotion until one of my co-workers asked me why I hadn't gotten it. Naturally, I was embarrassed to find out secondhand. More important, I was concerned because I would be reporting directly to someone with a big mouth who was boasting all around the organization about his appointment."

"When my boss told me I was invited to participate in an assessment center, I was really pleased. I thought to myself, 'Finally, management has recognized the job that I was doing.' However, I was nervous at the assessment center, and I normally don't perform well when somebody's watching me too closely. As a result, I was overly cautious in some of the group simulation exercises, and I screwed up the in-basket exercise.

"It was not until nearly three months after my participation in the assessment center that I received any feedback. My manager sat down with me and told me that he was sorry I had been judged to be nonpromotable. I asked him how he felt about that, and he told me it was not in his hands."

"My boss met with me and told me I had not been promoted. But she gave me a song-and-dance story loaded with platitudes, and never really told me why I didn't get the promotion or what my chances for promotion in the future were. She kept saying 'Don't worry about it. Your promotion will come through eventually.' Of course, that didn't make me feel any better."

In all three of these situations, managers failed to give adequate support and counseling to subordinates when they needed it most. Often managers avoid this important responsibility because they find it difficult and uncomfortable to give someone "bad news." Besides, they may feel somewhat guilty when a subordinate is bypassed for promotion. They don't know what to say, and whatever they do say usually is not said well—at a time when employees need their support the most.

The reason bypassed employees need extra attention and support is that they often feel they have to "do something" after they lose a promotion. Usually, this means escaping from a bad situation—going to another company. These feelings may be fostered by family members and co-workers who are disappointed that the employee did not get promoted.

Thus promotions may lead to dissatisfaction for both employees who are promoted and those who are not. Promotions affect everyone, not just the people directly involved.

COMMONSENSE ACTIONS

1. Always question your criteria in recommending subordinates for promotion. To aid in this questioning process, you should compare an employee's qualifications against a detailed job specification. If a job specification doesn't exist, gather sufficient information about the job opening so that you can do an intelligent job of matching.

If you have any doubts about an employee's ability to perform the duties required in the new job, give the employee a "tryout." If possible, arrange for the employee to take on some special assignments or even to spend some time in the other job.

In effect, the manager assumes responsibility for placing employees in positions in which they are likely to succeed. Too often, managers recommend employees for promotion as a reward for good performance. They aren't concerned about the ability of the employee to perform at a higher level.

2. If lateral opportunities do not exist in your organization, you should advocate them to higher management. In addition to the traditional movement "up the ladder," employees need other satisfying tracks to follow. I recommend a four-track system:

The traditional hierarchical track.

The specialty track.

The cross-functional track.

The general track.

With this four-track system, you can offer your employees alternatives. An employee might be promoted up the ladder. Or she might be assigned to a special job that is not at a higher level but that offers some status, extra income, and a change in responsibility. Or an employee might be assigned to a job at the same level in another department that also offers some recognition, status, job variety, and income advantages. Finally, an employee might be advanced in a general track. For example, the organization might have three or four grades of sales representative, engineer, accountant, and so on. Essentially, this general-track appointment recognizes the employee's job knowledge and ability to perform the job with less supervision.

3. A very important managerial responsibility is breaking the news to and counseling losers in a race for promotion. The form shown in Figure 18 can be helpful in carrying out this responsibility. It includes five key questions related to readiness for promotion, qualifications for promotion, and the impact of not being promoted on the

Figure 18. Counseling bypassed employees.

Name and Title

1. What are your immediate feelings about not being promoted?

2. Which of your qualifications for promotion may require
   strengthening?

3. What kind of training will help you get ready for promotion?

4. How long will it take you to get ready for promotion?

5. What actions are you planning to take as a result of
   having been passed by for promotion?

---

future of the employee. An open discussion of these questions can bring out the employee's feelings and give the
manager an opportunity to help the employee deal with
them. Here's a typical dialogue:

SUPERVISOR I know you feel angry at not being promoted
and think that I haven't evaluated your performance
fairly.

SUBORDINATE Can you blame me for feeling as I do? I've
been in this department longer than any other employee, and I've always worked hard and tried to do
my job well.

SUPERVISOR I know you work hard and genuinely try to do your best.

SUBORDINATE Then why didn't you promote me?

SUPERVISOR I would have liked to promote you because of your long service in the department. But in matching the job requirements with your qualifications, I realized that you hadn't closed important gaps that I, and my predecessors, have called to your attention.

SUBORDINATE I guess you're talking about the problems I have had meeting deadlines. (*Guided by the supervisor, the employee explores areas that have been holding him back and discusses ways in which he might overcome his deficiencies. If the deficiencies are not correctable, the supervisor must get the employee to confront that issue.*)

SUBORDINATE I've taken several courses in planning and management, and I want to be more organized and plan more effectively, but I just have trouble doing it.

SUPERVISOR Planning and organizing don't come easy for you?

SUBORDINATE That's right!

SUPERVISOR Since those skills are essential for advancement, it is likely that you will be passed by for promotion again in the future. How do you feel about that? (*The supervisor helps the employee understand that he has probably reached his level of competence and that he must adapt to that reality. Instead of getting angry at being passed by, he must learn to accept it and to focus on gaining satisfaction in his current work assignment.*)

4. Every manager should be an advocate for employees who are ready and qualified for promotion. If these employees have low-visibility jobs, the manager should investigate promotional opportunities that are available and recommend subordinates for these opportunities.

5. If your organization uses assessment centers to identify promotables, you have a dual responsibility. First, you should recommend employees for participation in the as-

sessment center who you feel are ready and qualified for promotion. There is an implied promise in being sent to an assessment center that the employee is being singled out for special consideration. Make sure you do not raise the hopes of employees who are almost certain to do poorly at the center.

Your second responsibility is to provide feedback after employees return from the assessment center. Generally, employees have a fair idea of how well they did even without the official assessment report. Listen to their comments and try to help them overcome any disappointments they may have.

CHAPTER 14

Supervision Problems

MANY of the personal reasons employees cite for leaving an organization are, in reality, manifestations of supervisory problems. These problems go unresolved because the employee and the supervisor don't recognize them. For example:

Ted quit because of "lack of challenge." The reason Ted wasn't challenged was that his supervisor had difficulty delegating to subordinates. The supervisor was niggardly in sharing his responsibilities. And even when he was forced to delegate, he never really let go completely.

Alice left because of what she described as an "unrelenting workload." This problem resulted from the failure of her immediate supervisor to distribute the work equitably. The supervisor failed to take action against weak performers. Instead, he transferred work from the weak performers to the strong performers. So the weak performers were, in effect, rewarded for not doing their jobs while the strong performers were punished for being productive.

Murray left an organization because he "wasn't learning anything new on the job." However, it was not the job, but the supervisor who was the root of the problem. The supervisor was a very conservative woman who resisted any changes in the scope of the work her employees performed. In addition, in the interests of protecting her subordinates, she limited their interactions with other departments. In the process, she stifled learning opportunities.

Nonsupportive and nonresponsive supervisors who turn away valued employees exhibit several common characteristics:

Failure to Set a Good Example
Nonsupportive supervisors do not set a good example. Often the reason is that they have become immobilized by fear. Rather than focusing on how they perform the job, they are concerned with how they look to top management, and they worry about whether subordinates are doing anything that could make them look bad. This preoccupation with self-protection inspires neither respect nor confidence. Subordinates can't look up to a supervisor who is forever groveling.

Inflexible Work Style
Supervisors may turn away employees because they fail to adapt their leadership style to the needs of the people

they are supervising and the demands of the situation. Accordingly, they either underlead or overlead, and in the process they frustrate and alienate subordinates. For example:

The department head in an accounting group was strongly task-oriented. His primary concern was completing assigned projects on time, no matter what the human cost. He expected employees to follow his example. And he worked extraordinarily long hours and frequently took work home.

The supervisor created extra work for himself and others. Although his subordinates were knowledgeable, experienced, and committed to doing a good job, he supervised them closely, insisting that they check regularly with him to report their progress. As a result, a considerable amount of time was wasted talking about projects rather than doing them. And since the supervisor was a perfectionist, time was wasted going over inconsequential details.

Another supervisor in the same organization had an "underleading" work style that also bred employee dissatisfaction. The director of data processing was the complete opposite of the accounting director. He concerned himself primarily with his relationships with subordinates. He was described as "a really nice guy who could never get anything done." He was so busy smoothing over relationships that the department was continually in hot water with the groups it serviced.

Some of his subordinates were not knowledgeable and experienced and not committed to doing the job. They needed firm leadership from him. However, he usually failed to take any firm action because he was fearful of upsetting his subordinates. His inability to adapt his leadership style to the situation created the very problems he was trying to avoid.

Indecisiveness

Employees find it difficult to work for managers who can't make up their minds. Here's how one employee described the conditions created by her indecisive manager:

"We spend half our time waiting for the boss to make decisions. He would always send us back to study the problem some more, and to gather facts that he supposedly needed to make a decision but that were really unnecessary. Projects were prolonged, and we had to put in overtime to meet deadlines that should have posed no problem at all.

"As a result of his indecisiveness, the whole group acquired a bad reputation. So nobody was considered for promotional openings in other departments, and none of the special projects that we all wanted were ever assigned to our group. No wonder we had such a high turnover rate."

Unfairness

A supervisor turns away employees when they judge him to be "unfair." Naturally, this doesn't mean that he's unfair all the time. But it does mean that he is unfair a sufficient number of times that his subordinates believe "that's the way he is."

Employees continually keep score, questioning everything the supervisor says and does:

"Did he give me a fair salary increase?"
"Did he rate my performance fairly?"
"Is he distributing the workload fairly?"
"Is he more demanding of me than of others?"
"Is his criticism fair?"
"Did he discipline me fairly?"

An accumulation of "no" answers can undermine morale and lead to turnover.

Noncommunicativeness

Employees feel insecure when they are kept in the dark. They want to be informed continually about where they stand and what is happening in the department. When a supervisor is secretive or just doesn't do a good job of keeping her unit informed, subordinates tend to fill in the information gaps with gossip and rumors that add to their insecurity.

A supervisor's communication deficiencies can also hinder employees' job performance, leading to unrest and dissatisfaction. For example, the supervisor may not explain work assignments clearly or may fail to supply sufficient information to complete assignments properly. As a result, employees' performance is compromised.

The impact of a supervisor's noncommunicativeness was described to me as follows:

"My boss never told me what to do, and I had to muddle along by myself. Naturally, because I had insufficient training and experience, I made mistakes. Yet my boss would never accept any blame for my mistakes. She gave me low performance ratings and minimal salary increases. Yet she was actually surprised when I said I was quitting."

Collapse Under Stress

Supervisors who can't handle stress pass it on to their subordinates. When they overreact or panic, they create extra work for employees. And they leave subordinates leaderless just when they need direction and support the most.

When a department is operating under extreme pressure, the level of work satisfaction tends to be higher if managers are able to cope with the stress. Managers can put things in perspective for employees and give them the comforting feeling that they are being fully supported during "hard times."

Destructive Criticism

A basic supervisory function that is frequently abused is criticism. Naturally, the supervisor must bring to the attention of subordinates things that they are doing wrong that affect their performance. However, many supervisors do not use sound judgment in deciding what, when, and how to criticize.

If any of your subordinates sound like this former employee of a major company, you may be turning them away with destructive criticism:

"I don't mind a reasonable amount of criticism. In fact, I expect it. But my boss was a nitpicker. He criticized everything and anything. After a while, I just stopped listening to anything he said, but that didn't seem to make any difference to him. I got the feeling that he really didn't expect me to change my behavior, and that he criticized just to prove he was boss and was watching me carefully."

Negative Reinforcement

Supervisors may, without realizing it, teach subordinates that it doesn't pay to be enthusiastic and committed to the job. They teach this discouraging lesson by failing to reinforce subordinates' extra effort and initiative. For example, when subordinates are excited about a project and invest a great deal of time—including personal time—in it, they expect a supervisor to appreciate their efforts and, at the very least, to acknowledge the work they have put into the project. Instead, the supervisor may say nothing at all or give a perfunctory acknowledgment.

Supervisors take the joy out of the job by making comments like these:

"What's the big deal? That's what you get paid for doing."
"Not bad."

"That's all right, but. . . ."

"Why did you waste all that time doing that?"

Hogging the Credit

Unsung heroes leave for organizations that will recognize their accomplishments. The supervisor who tells subordinates, "Don't worry about pleasing anybody else; I'll take care of you," robs them of the pride of ownership and denies them recognition that is rightfully theirs.

Typical of complaints about supervisors who hog the credit are these comments by a young engineer:

"I just couldn't understand my ex-boss. He was a capable engineer himself, with a good work record. Yet he presented every good idea from our work group as if it were his own. We were never allowed to present our own ideas outside the department. Even though he treated me well and gave me top performance ratings and salary increases, I felt he was hiding me in the closet. I wanted other people in the company to know that I was a creative engineer with lots of ideas."

Depersonalizing Employees

Subordinates have individual desires and needs, and want them to be recognized. The supervisor who gives all subordinates "equal treatment" in the interest of fairness may cause serious problems. Here are just some of the cases in which "equal treatment" doesn't work:

- Employees with unequal capabilities should not be given equal work assignments.
- Employees with the same length of service in a job but unequal performance should not be given the same rewards.
- Employees with unequal interest in a special work assignment should not be treated alike.

o Employees with an unequal commitment to work should not get equal rewards.

Sometimes supervisors become so concerned about not exhibiting favoritism that they take a step in the opposite direction: even when there are sound reasons to favor one subordinate over another, they don't do so.

All these characteristics of nonsupportive supervisors can have a major impact on turnover. Yet organizations often support these "high turnover" supervisors for much longer than they should. Typically, the rationalization is, "That's just the way he is. He's done good work for us for a long time, and we didn't realize how much damage he was doing."

No organization can afford supervisors who drive away valuable employees. To accept them is dangerous, to ignore them is foolhardy, and to support them doesn't make any sense at all!

COMMONSENSE ACTION

1. As a supervisor, the most important attribute you can possess is introspection. Unless you monitor your own behavior, you will be unable to correct your mistakes. The form shown in Figure 19 can assist you in your self-evaluation. I suggest you complete it at least once a year. Also, you might ask trusted subordinates to complete it independently, commenting on your supervisory style. Then, compare their answers with yours.

2. Encourage and solicit feedback from subordinates. You can do this formally, using some of the feedback instruments described in previous chapters, or informally when opportunities present themselves.

3. When feedback is offered by subordinates, always appear to be completely *accepting*. This doesn't mean that you agree automatically with subordinates' comments, but you should listen carefully and try to understand them. Reserve judgment on what is being said.

Figure 19. Manager's self-evaluation form.

	Regularly 5 points	Occasionally 2 points	Rarely 1 point
1. Am I genuinely helpful to subordinates?			
2. Do I set a good example?			
3. Do I assign reasonable responsibility and clear accountability?			
4. Do I give constructive criticism in bite-size amounts?			
5. Do I reinforce good behavior?			
6. Do I hog all the credit?			
7. Do I give subordinates a say in decisions that affect them?			
8. Do I give adequate support?			
9. Am I fair?			
10. Do I communicate clearly?			
11. Am I open in my communications?			
12. Am I decisive?			
13. Do I give objective performance appraisals?			

Figure 19. Manager's self-evaluation form (continued).

	Regularly 5 points	Occasionally 2 points	Rarely 1 point
14. Are my expectations for subordinates realistic?			
15. Do I acknowledge the individuality of subordinates?			

A score above 60 is high. The manager is supplying effective supervision.

A score between 40 and 60 is fair. The "rarely" answers are weaknesses.

A score below 40 is low. The manager's supervisory behavior is self-defeating.

4. In responding to legitimate criticism from subordinates, you must be willing to change. You can't persist in a supervisory style that turns away employees.

5. Enlist subordinates in helping you to change. A friendly reminder from subordinates, "You asked me to tell you when you . . ." can help you reverse a long-ingrained work style.

6. You may find it helpful to carry around an "I did it again" book. I use a 3″ × 5″ notebook in which I record any of my I-wish-I-had-handled-the-situation-differently behaviors. For example:

When   October 10, 1980

What   I didn't back up John C.

Where   At the weekly interdepartmental meeting.

Who   Besides John C., I believe Tom E. and Mary S. were upset by my actions.

Why   I was embarrassed to admit that John C. had discussed the project with me, but I hadn't paid enough attention to what he told me.

7. Practice situational leadership. In the changing work situations you face daily, continually ask yourself, "How much supervision is necessary in this situation? Are my subordinates capable of, and committed to, performing assigned tasks with minimal or no supervision from me?"

8. Use positive reinforcement whenever possible. If you want employees to do the "right" things, you have to make sure their behavior is rewarded. Often your acknowledgment that a task was done properly is reward enough. At other times, stronger reinforcements may be necessary. You have to know your employees well enough to identify the kinds of rewards they need. And always give immediate rewards, following closely the behavior that you are acknowledging.

9. Raise your expectations about your subordinates. Researchers have documented that employees tend to fulfill their supervisors' expectations. Many employees would be capable of much stronger performance if they were supported rather than "written off" by their managers.

10. Become more aware of your own hangups. In particular, question the way you supervise minorities and older employees. The tendency to give them *special* treatment affects them and other employees. Favoritism makes people feel they can do no wrong and they sometimes become careless. In addition, other people develop resentment or become jealous.

The impressions you form of subordinates in the first 30 days of employment often affect how you supervise them thereafter. And many of these first impressions are colored by stereotypical thinking. For example, if you believe women are more emotional than men, you are likely to "read" emotionality into a new female employee's behavior during her first few weeks on the job.

11. Recognize the unspoken psychological contract that exists between you and your subordinates. If you want subordinates to deliver what you expect from them, you too have to deliver. Many managers do not recognize this

psychological contract and unknowingly violate it. Although a psychological contract doesn't appear in writing, both employees and employers generally know what is expected of each other. The employee, of course, is expected to supply a full day's work, and in return he expects fair compensation. And, if the employee performs outstandingly, after a reasonable time in grade he expects a promotion. That's why during exit interviews employees frequently cite violations of the psychological contract—which are strongly denied by supervisors—as a reason for leaving.

12. Search for grievances. A popular saying is, "Why look for trouble?" I would amend that statement to read, "Why look for trouble when it's too late to do anything about it?" Managers should look for trouble *before* it starts. They should be sensitive to developing grievances and other problems and recognize them early enough to take action.

The strongest weapon you can use against turnover is direct, regular contact with subordinates. Supervisory actions often determine whether valued employees stay or leave the organization. While you may not be able to erase any of the mistakes you make, you may be able to soften their effects. Most important, by regularly reviewing the entries in your "I did it again" book, you will be more aware of patterns and less likely to repeat your errors.

CHAPTER 15

Growth Problems

MOST employees need to feel a sense of personal growth throughout their careers. As with all living organisms, when growth stops vitality declines.

The symptoms of arrested growth are highly visible in employees getting ready to leave an organization:

- They have low energy.
- They lack enthusiasm.
- They lack commitment.
- They're disinterested in their work assignment.
- They're chronic complainers.
- They're cynical.

○ They know things are not the same as they were in the past, and they feel differently about the organization and their job.

What's changed for the worse for these employees is the realization that they have nothing to look forward to. They no longer feel they can say, "My job gets better all the time. I'm learning, developing, increasing my responsibility—growing."

THE ROLE OF TRAINING IN PERSONAL GROWTH

Growth in many organizations is front-ended. Training is invested most heavily in beginners. Supervisors devote much of their attention to trainees. Thus the consequence of learning a job rapidly and well is to receive less training and supervisory attention. For many employees this loss of attention makes the job far less desirable. As one sales representative described the feeling:

"My first year with the organization was extremely challenging and exciting. I received intensive training, coming to the home office for formal instruction for a total of six weeks on three different trips. My manager spent a lot of time with me, sharing with me the know-how he had acquired over the years. The training department kept in continual communication with me, sending me all kinds of educational material.

"I put in a lot of personal time. I felt I was making an investment in myself, learning and developing new skills. However, after the first year the training stopped abruptly. And my manager shifted his attention to training and developing the newer employees. As a result, the job was far less stimulating and satisfying."

Besides being front-ended, training is usually designed to teach job essentials only. But employees often want to learn more than the essentials. For example, in the pharmaceuticals industry, sales representatives are given superb training in product knowledge and, to a lesser extent, training in selling skills. However, they receive little training beyond that. As a result of this narrow training, after just two or three years in the job pharmaceuticals sales representatives often get the feeling that they are "not growing." They recognize that they are not developing the kinds of skills they will need to perform at higher-level jobs or in other functional areas of the organization.

Most training beyond technical training is general in nature, rather than individualized, and is often "canned." Employees are trained in such subjects as time management, problem solving, and the currently fashionable transactional analysis. They may or may not be interested in the topic, and it may or may not address their needs.

Not only are these training programs likely to contribute minimally to employees' sense of growth, but they may even lead to dissatisfaction. The competitive environment of many training programs can create stress and ill-feelings. Valued employees may feel that they are being "put on the spot." Or they may find the training material so basic that they feel it "insulting" to present it to them.

Most employees do not perceive traditional training as being something "for them." Instead, it's something they must do to be able to perform their jobs. And it's something that is observed by superiors, who may decide they haven't done it well. They realize, too, that poor training performance can hurt their careers. For example, the management development program in one organization was notorious for "stopping cold" the careers of promising managers. The program featured a simulation exercise that was carefully observed by trainers and members of higher management, who "dropped in" occasionally during the exercise. If the trainees received negative comments, they knew from the experience of colleagues that it was time to look for another job.

As a manager, you should be aware of the role of training in contributing to employees' feelings of personal growth. You should also take a hard look at your commitment to the personal development of employees. When you assume responsibility for helping subordinates grow, you should adopt the role of facilitator, helping them overcome the inertia that prevents them from launching self-development programs. You provide objectivity, insights, and the benefits of your own experience. Your continuing interest and guidance are essential to the success of any development program.

Managers often make a weak commitment to the personal development of subordinates. Generally, a "what's in it for me" attitude prevails. While training may yield immediate benefits, the benefits of development tend to be long-term and much less apparent. Many employees, particularly those who decide to leave the organization, recognize the lack of commitment of managers to subordinates' personal development. The manager's attitude is manifested in an unwillingness to support development efforts with time and money and, even more important, in a lack of reinforcement of a subordinate's personal development efforts. For example:

o In a company with a very large sales force, educational support is provided only for specific technical subjects.

o In several organizations that supposedly encourage personal development, it's virtually impossible to get time off to attend even company-sponsored programs. Employees find it discouraging and frustrating to register for a program only to find that work demands force cancellation.

Personal development may become an especially acute issue when employees work under supervisors who are uninterested in offering development assistance or who are even opposed to developing subordinates. The complaints of subordinates working under these managers sound alike from organization to organization:

"To my boss, I was just a machine. He expected me to perform mechanically from day to day, ignoring my needs and aspirations. Naturally, I had no chance to learn anything under him."

"My boss was always complaining about something I did wrong, yet he would not take the time to show me how to correct my deficiencies. And at performance appraisals he would tell me, 'You're a poor communicator,' or 'You don't know how to manage your time.' But he didn't tell me what to do about it."

"My boss didn't want me to grow because she was afraid I would outgrow my current job. She considered me to be vital to the smooth functioning of the department and was determined not to lose me. So she did not help me develop my skills, and discouraged anything I did on my own."

Fortunately, with or without assistance, employees experience personal growth. They make the most of the learning experiences they are provided and search out other experiences themselves. As a result of this continuing development, they are capable of and anxious to assume greater responsibility.

However, their companies often seem to be indifferent to the gains they have made. Typically, employees express their feelings about this lack of response as follows:

"I can't understand it. The company paid for my education as a programmer. When I completed a two-year course with honors, I expected a change in status on the job. Yet I wasn't given any programming assignments. Instead, management continued to hire new programmers, claiming that the company needed experienced people. But how was I supposed to get experience if I wasn't given a chance?"

"I'm the first one to admit that when I joined the organization I was immature, and some of my values were inappropriate in a business environment. However, I feel I demonstrated substantial personal growth in a relatively short period of time. Even so, my boss treated me just the same."

CONSEQUENCES OF BLOCKED PERSONAL GROWTH

Although "running in place" may be acceptable to some employees, it is a source of pain to many others. They may feel embarrassment and guilt at their lack of growth and at "falling behind" co-workers. Certainly, they will experience disappointment and frustration. In some cases, their unhappiness may lead to mental health problems, alcoholism, and drug abuse. Other employees appear unconcerned about their lack of growth. They rationalize what's happening, claiming that it's only temporary or that they are really not interested in growing on the job because they have other interests.

Thus, while employees who feel concern that their personal growth is blocked are candidates for voluntary turnover, employees who are unconcerned about their growth may become candidates for involuntary turnover. When employees no longer grow on the job, it becomes increasingly difficult for them to maintain interest and commitment. So if the employees don't leave voluntarily, their performance may drop to the point where remedial action has to be taken.

The much talked about "midcareer crisis" is explainable to a large extent by an employee's sense of arrested growth. The employee feels, "I have grown out of this job and want to do something that is completely new and different." The midcareer crisis can occur at all job levels and may begin as early as the thirties. It depends on how much personal growth an employee wants to achieve and his or her perception of how much growth the job and the organization offer.

COMMONSENSE ACTIONS

1. Demonstrate a commitment to the personal development of your subordinates by investing your own time in it. Encourage and facilitate employee participation in development programs within and outside the organization.

2. At least annually, preferably in conjunction with the performance appraisal, help your subordinates plan self-improvement programs. As an aid, you might use the self-improvement form in Figure 20. For illustrative purposes, a program for a sales representative is shown.

First, the manager and sales representative review the essential job requirements, including such areas as technical knowledge, participating in sales meetings, recordkeeping, and planning territory coverage (column 1). Then, with the assistance of the manager, the subordinate evaluates what he does well, what gives him some trouble, and what he does poorly (columns 2–4). Manager and subordinate then discuss learning activities that will help the subordinate develop skills, such as subscribing to trade journals, taking a public speaking course, and seeking help from other sales representatives. Subsequently, the subordinate lists the actions he is taking to improve and notes the progress he is making (columns 5–6). As the subordinate completes these new learning activities, the manager should give immediate positive reinforcement.

3. As employees grow, you should acknowledge their growth and try to make use of their new strengths and skills. If possible, assign more responsibility, even if the assignment is not permanent. You might give employees special projects or assign them to problem-solving teams. At the very least, you should demonstrate that you value subordinates' advice by consulting with them regularly.

4. Establish an ongoing dialogue with employees, trying to determine to what extent they feel they are learning and developing within their current job assignments. Here's how you might initiate a dialogue on the subject and some of the key questions you might ask:

Figure 20. Planning a self-improvement program.

(1) Essential Job Requirements	(2) What I Do Well	(3) What Gives Me Some Trouble	(4) What I Do Poorly	(5) What I'm Doing to Improve	(6) What Progress I'm Making
Technical Knowledge	X			Subscribing to trade journals	Keeping up to date
Participating in Sales Meetings			X	Taking public speaking course; joined Toastmasters' Club	3/15 Favorable comments from boss at sales meeting 6/20 Made well-received special presentation
Recordkeeping		X		Asking for help from other sales representatives	9/10 Using methods of other sales representatives; my records are now in good condition
Planning Territory Coverage		X		Review current procedures with manager	1/5 Started to implement revised coverage plan 4/20 Revised plan working well

MANAGER Anything new happening on the job?

SUBORDINATE Nothing—the same old thing!

MANAGER Just the same old routine?

SUBORDINATE Well, except for the new cost reduction project.

MANAGER What have you learned from it? (*Manager and*

subordinate explore the nonroutine things the subordinate has worked on recently.)

MANAGER It sounds like some of the routine is getting you down and you'd like to do something else. *(Manager and subordinate explore new activities that would be mutually beneficial.)*

MANAGER Now that we have agreed on some things that you might be able to do, do you think that you are ready for them?

SUBORDINATE Well, I'm going to need help getting started on some of the projects, and I may need some special training.

MANAGER Let's talk about how I might be able to help you or arrange for training either inside or outside the organization. *(Manager and subordinate decide on new development needs and resources.)*

5. Learn to appreciate and take pride in your role as a developer of other people. The productivity of your subordinates may be directly related to the interest you show in their development and the time you invest in it. Remember, the burden of development falls heavily on you. After employees have completed their initial training and have moved into midcareer, they may need even more of your time and attention.

Personal growth is a joint responsibility: both yours and the employee's. Neither of you can afford to ignore that responsibility.

PART THREE

EARLY

DIAGNOSIS

This part of the book focuses on preparedness: avoiding surprises.

Turnover is a surprise only to unprepared managers who fail to recognize the warning signals and who do not take reasonable precautions. Chapter 16 discusses the value of setting up an early-warning system and describes a series of warning indicators. Chapter 17 shows managers how to minimize the impact of turnover through human resources planning. Emphasis is placed on the realistic appraisal of the cost and difficulty of replacing employees and on establishing the "market value" of current employees as the basis for salary adjustments.

CHAPTER 16

The Early-Warning System

ORGANIZATIONS collect data about turnover *after* the fact. While such information is useful in diagnosing problems that contributed to turnover, it is of little value in dealing with current problems.

An early-warning system is needed to pinpoint developing problems at a time when it is still possible to take corrective action. For example, using the *critical incident log,* described later in this chapter, one manager realized that several of his subordinates were concerned about recent procedural changes. He called them together to discuss the issue and learned that the changes placed an extraordinary burden on them, much more than on other people in the organization. In fact, two of the subordinates were so upset that they were actively looking for other employment, and two other subordinates were seriously considering either making an intracompany transfer or starting an employment search outside the company. Recognizing the urgency of the problem, the manager was able to take remedial action and saved all four employees.

Not all managers are as sensitive to incidents that employees perceive as significant. Sometimes, in expressing their concern, employees do not reveal the depth of their feeling. Perhaps they are embarrassed to do so or assume that their manager already knows what's bothering them.

Managers usually give passing attention to employee concerns and resolve to consider the employees' problems "when they get time." But the significance of the problems fades as the managers occupy themselves with other matters. Even when employees bring up the same concerns repeatedly over a period of time, managers don't recognize that they are dealing with the same problem and that it is probably becoming more serious. For example:

A talented and highly valued quality control engineer caused considerable difficulty in an organization when he resigned. No one in the organization was prepared to take his place, and it was difficult to find a qualified replacement without an extensive search. The general manager called me in as a consultant in the hope of avoiding such "costly surprises" in the future.

When I interviewed the manager of the quality control department, he told me he had had no indication that the quality control engineer was going to leave. I then interviewed the engineer, who reported that over a period of two years he had complained on several occasions about the extraordinary work demands the growth of business was creating, and the need he had for an assistant.

In further discussions the engineer acknowledged that he may not have conveyed the depth of his feelings to his supervisor. And the department head acknowledged that he had not given sufficient attention to the request from his subordinate and had not realized the number of times his subordinate had requested help. Both, too late, realized that the issue could have been resolved and that, in retrospect, the resignation had hurt both the engineer and the company.

Whatever is important to employees deserves attention. Otherwise, problems become magnified in importance, because they come to represent "managers who don't give a damn about their subordinates." Yet often all the managers had to do to diffuse these problems was to give them a fair hearing and to watch for further developments.

A common source of complaints about lack of a "fair hearing" is the annual performance appraisal interview. When an employee's performance is *officially* evaluated, differences of opinion are bound to arise. Nobody wants to be told that he is not performing as well as he thinks he is. Unfortunately, differences in opinions are often unresolved. After an extended point-counter-point discussion, a manager will usually say, "That's my rating of your performance. Since I'm the boss, you'll have to accept it." And the subordinate says, "I guess I have no choice. I'm disappointed, but I'll accept the rating."

Generally, the manager then forgets about the subordinate's disappointment and doesn't stay alert to further developments. In the meanwhile, the subordinate's bad feelings may get stronger, destroying his relationship with the supervisor and making him dissatisfied with his job and the organization.

Grievance handling is another area in which unresolved issues can escalate into serious problems. Managers tend to underestimate the importance of grievances and the emotional investment employees make in them. By ignoring grievances or handling them perfunctorily, managers turn them into significant issues. For example:

In one company grievances about parking rules set into motion a chain of events that led to the resignation of valued employees. A dispute arose over who would be assigned reserved parking spaces. Several department heads requested spaces for their subordinates. However, one department head didn't want to be bothered and didn't submit a request for spaces. His subordinates complained, and he pushed the matter aside.

When the spaces were assigned to other departments, several of his subordinates were very upset. They felt that he hadn't supported them. As they discussed what happened among themselves, they concluded that they could not count on their supervisor's support in the future. As a result, three subordinates eventually left the organization.

Managers aren't always given an opportunity to resolve grievances. Often employees keep them to themselves. Perhaps they are fearful of confrontations. Or they think, "What's the use? Nobody will listen to us." So they discuss the grievances with each other, blowing them out of proportion and spreading dissatisfaction.

Unresolved issues related to career development can also lead to dissatisfaction. Employees frequently address career concerns to managers. However, they often find that the managers are not knowledgeable about career opportunities and are unwilling to supply any real career guidance. Employees' feelings about inept career counseling were summed up by this disgruntled financial analyst:

"When I tried to talk to my boss about my future, he hemmed and hawed and told me nothing. Except for supplying some obvious information, he offered virtually nothing about job opportunities or about qualifications for available jobs. To make matters worse, he lectured to me on being impatient, overambitious, and overly concerned with the future."

No matter how perfect a work environment is, employees find things to become concerned about—critical incidents, differences in opinion about performance appraisals, grievances, lack of career guidance. Many of these concerns have the potential to grow unless they are dealt with early and appropriately. Unrecognized and unresolved, they can become time bombs, waiting to explode.

COMMONSENSE ACTIONS

To detect unresolved issues, managers might want to build the following early-warning system. It employs five warning indicators of developing problems:

1. The *critical incident log* is a permanent record of significant interactions between the manager and members of staff. It demonstrates to employees that the manager thinks enough of them to recall anything significant that happens between them. A critical incident log is relatively easy to maintain. I recommend a small looseleaf notebook, divided into separate sections for each person you regularly deal with. Record the entries chronologically and in ink. The format of an entry is shown in Figure 21. You should describe each incident in detail, answering such questions as:

- What happened?
- When did it happen?
- Did the same thing or anything similar happen in the past?
- Who was involved?
- What led up to it?
- What feelings were expressed or what did you infer from what was said?

After carefully describing the incident, note the potential consequences. What might happen if you don't take any action? Then analyze the situation in terms of the following:

- How have you and the other parties contributed to the problem?
- How can they contribute to the solution?
- To what extent are misunderstandings and differing perceptions contributing to the problem?

Figure 21. Critical incident log.

1. *Description*
   Today I talked to Joy Evans about her sloppy recordkeeping. I've mentioned recordkeeping deficiencies to her in
   the past, but I didn't make an issue of them. This time I
   was more critical and direct.

2. *Potential Consequences*
   Joy is very sensitive to criticism, and she's probably upset
   about what I said. But if she doesn't keep better records, it
   could lead to a serious problem.

3. *Analysis*
   I've contributed to the problem by not fully explaining
   the importance of good recordkeeping and the serious
   consequences of incomplete or sloppy records. Joy has
   contributed to the problem because, by her own admis-
   sion, she thought recordkeeping was a waste of time and
   that I wasn't really concerned about it.

4. *Proposed Action*
   I'll go over good recordkeeping standards with her and
   ask her to check her own records regularly for adherence
   to standards. I'll spot-check her records every other week
   or so.

   ○ To what extent are forces beyond the control of the
     parties influencing the problem?
   ○ How likely is it that the situation can be improved in
     the near future?

Finally, record your proposed action—the immediate
and long-term steps you plan to take as a result of the
critical incident.

Since it is essential to follow up on any critical incident,
you should keep an additional record, as shown in Figure
22. Maintain this in a separate section of the notebook,
divided by month, so that it serves as your tickler file. List
the proposed actions and their scheduled and actual com-
pletion dates. File the pages by scheduled dates and check
them every week or so.

Figure 22. Follow-up tickler file.

Item: Joy Evans, sloppy recordkeeping. March 1, 1980.		
Proposed Action	Scheduled Completion Date	Actual Completion Date
Review and agree on standards	March 2, 1980	March 2, 1980
Spot-check	March 16, 1980 April 6, 1980	March 19, 1980

When writing entries in your log, be brief and use simple prose. The record is meant only to help you recall the details of a critical incident. It should take less than 15 minutes to record a typical entry. And you should record only those incidents that may have future importance. Typical examples include grievances, personal disputes, career discussions, compensation problems, and performance deficiency or disciplinary discussions.

The following cases demonstrate how well a critical incident log works.

Jill had a reputation in the department as a trouble-maker. Her supervisor had recorded two incidents in the logbook over a six-month period in which Jill was the center of a departmental squabble. When a third incident occurred and Jill tried to blame the other party, as she had in the past, her supervisor referred to the other log entries. Those entries were convincing evidence that Jill's provocative behavior had caused similar problems with other people in the past. More important, they were enough to get Jill to address her own shortcomings.

A supervisor was upset with a worker's untidy bench

area. Whenever she complained about it, the employee invariably came up with a variety of excuses, citing unusual work demands that interfered with routine maintenance. After recording several similar incidents in the critical incident log, the supervisor confronted the employee again. When the excuses started, the supervisor challenged them and documented her case with the hard facts from the logbook.

An employee finally drew up enough courage to speak with her supervisor about her concern that she was in a dead-end job. Several months later a promotion developed, and after reviewing the logbook the supervisor called in the employee to discuss it with her. In the course of the discussion, the supervisor was able to play back some of the employees' feelings from the earlier conversation. Although the employee didn't get the promotion, she was very pleased that her supervisor thought enough about her to remember what she had said. The experience greatly strengthened their relationship.

As these cases reveal, a critical incident log can serve you in many ways. Its value is derived from the universal human need to be heard—to feel that when we talk, others listen and remember what we say. But instead of burdening your memory and risking inaccurate recall, you can establish a written record. It takes only a small investment of time to guarantee an accurate, permanent record of a critical incident.

2. To reconcile differences of opinion about performance ratings, you might establish a *court of appeal.* A staff member could serve in this capacity, or your own supervisor could conduct a second-level review. Or you could schedule a second performance review meeting, giving the subordinate sufficient time to prepare his or her appeal for an upgraded rating. While employees may not be able to influence a change in rating, at least they should have an opportunity to receive a fair hearing and a full explanation of the basis on which they were rated.

3. To help employees feel that they can bring grievances to your attention with impunity, appoint a *rotating ombudsman* in your work group. For a specified period of time, generally six months, a staff member assumes the responsibility of serving as a clearinghouse for worker grievances. The ombudsman checks with co-workers regularly, asking about any developing problems. Urgent problems are brought to the immediate attention of the manager; all other problems are reviewed at a regular monthly meeting. All grievances are anonymous—unless it is necessary to identify the source of a complaint and the ombudsman has received permission to do so.

One of the advantages of this system is that it promotes more productive discussions of grievances than the usual "gripe" sessions among employees. Often, just talking it over with a co-worker may change an employee's view of a perceived inequity.

4. One technique that many organizations have used effectively to uncover grievances is the *circular letter*. An open letter like the one shown in Figure 23 is sent to a member of the staff, who records his reply anonymously. The letter is then sent to another member of the staff, who records her reply anonymously. When the last member of the staff has recorded a reply, the letter is forwarded to the manager, who summarizes the results and sends them to all members of the staff for comment.

5. To give employees an opportunity to express their career concerns, you can create a *career development center* in your office or any other readily accessible location. The career development center offers employees a chance to obtain career information and to talk about their futures. To build the center, you should collect information on the following subjects:

- Next career step opportunities for employees, both within the department and in other departments.
- Job requirements and specifications.
- Supply and demand for different categories of jobs.
- Job descriptions.

When employees come to you with career concerns, you

Figure 23. Circular letter.

Dear Staff Member:

Your satisfaction with the work environment is of concern to you, to me, and to the organization. Yet you may occasionally feel that either I or the organization has done something that lessens your satisfaction.

When that happens, I hope that you will bring it to my attention. However, I know that for personal reasons you may feel uncomfortable about doing so. This letter gives you an opportunity to express your feelings anonymously.

After recording your comments, please pass on the letter to my secretary, who will route it to another co-worker. When all the members of the staff have expressed their concerns, I will summarize their comments and send them to you. In this way, you will learn whether your feelings are shared by co-workers and will be able to offer additional comments.

Naturally, I will be responsive to any of the concerns expressed by members of my staff.

Sincerely,

Department Manager

---

are now in a position to discuss future job alternatives, the requirements for these jobs, and the probability of obtaining them. You can also provide a description of the jobs and guidance on how to qualify for them.

Some managers feel, "It's not my job to conduct career discussions. I refer my subordinates to personnel." However, managers who relinquish responsibility in this area demonstrate to subordinates that they are not interested in their careers. At that point career concerns assume greater importance, and may lead to turnover.

CHAPTER 17

Human Resources Planning

EVERY manager needs to be supported by an ample supply of good employees. In order to meet continually changing work demands, the manager must maintain an adequate staff at all times. This process of matching work demands and employees is called human resources planning.

Human resources planning consists of three major activities. The first is forecasting human resources needs. The second is assessing potential turnover. The third is providing for organizational renewal. All three of these activities, taken together, have considerable impact on the vitality of an organization and the satisfaction of its employees.

FORECASTING HUMAN RESOURCES

Managers must be able to forecast potential surpluses or shortages in human resources so they can take steps to avoid staffing problems in the most effective and least costly way. To make this forecast, managers first need to know how long-range corporate plans will affect their own business unit. Some of the critical questions about the future that they will have to consider include:

- At what rate is our business growing or declining?
- What products are being added and what products are being dropped?
- What new technology will be introduced—and do we have the capability to supply that technology?

Besides reviewing corporate long-range plans, managers should monitor trends in their unit's workload and project them into the future. If a business unit is consistently asked to deliver more man-hours than its available capacity, forcing overtime and weekend work, the unit is understaffed.

Many managers are reluctant to admit that they are understaffed because of the problems that adding staff poses in the company. So they suffer silently until the understaffing creates substantial problems. For example, in one organization, a series of resignations within a department went unnoticed until an anonymous letter was sent to the corporate president complaining about the "extraordinary work demands." The staff members in the department were often required to work until 8:00 or 9:00 P.M. every day, and to work a full day on Saturdays. As a result, many of them were exhausted and were upset because the job was "ruining their home life."

In monitoring workload trends, a manager may discover that the work unit has a capacity in excess of work demands. Rather than hoping that "no one will notice," the manager should plan a staff cutback, and should do so far enough in advance to find new work assignments for surplus employees and thus avoid a layoff. For example, the growth of a business unit responsible for marketing a mature product line began to plateau. Recognizing the slowdown and the impact it would have on his staff, the manager of the unit prepared a skills inventory of his employees and confidentially circulated it to managers in other departments. IIe was careful not to try to "dump" his worst performers. Instead, he matched the skills of his employees with the needs of other department managers. As a result, he was successful in placing all his excess personnel within a six-month period.

Besides being concerned about surpluses and shortages, managers should anticipate the impact of technological change on their staff. The skills of employees may become obsolete, requiring retraining or replacement. Thus a manager may have an adequate "head count," yet not be able to satisfy the requirements of changing technology. For example, the incoming director of an engineering research and development group had to replace half the members of the current staff because they were unable to keep up with technological demands. When I questioned him about these terminations, he indicated that all the terminated employees could have been retrained, but the previous director didn't recognize the need early enough and the new director didn't have the time to retrain them now. So he had to hire engineers from the outside whose skills were up to date.

PREDICTING TURNOVER

When forecasting human resources needs, managers usually focus on additions and cutbacks, paying no attention to anticipated movements out of the work unit—turnover. Typically their reasoning is, "I can only guess who may quit and who will stay."

Managers don't have to "guess" about turnover if they

systematically record significant data about employees' intentions. They should regularly collect data on the following items:

- Who's been in the job long enough to start thinking about a job change?
- At the employee's current age, what's likely to be happening in his or her life that might precipitate a job change?
- Who's affected most by recent changes in the work environment?
- What critical incidents may cause an employee to reevaluate his or her current job status?
- How marketable in the labor market are the talents of the employees on staff?
- What changes in performance may signal changes in an employee's feelings about the job and the company?

To demonstrate how to systematically assess the intentions of employees, let's review a case history. In this case, the manager completed a vulnerability analysis, as described in Chapter 3, and maintained a *critical incident log,* as described in Chapter 15:

Because Bob Allen was only 28 years old and already had a responsible job as the director of training, his manager watched his career development closely. The manager knew that Bob was very ambitious. He also knew that even though Bob had been in the job for only two years, he might be considering a job change because of recent events in his personal life. Bob's wife, who had a high-paying job, resigned to give birth to their first child. In addition, Bob had just purchased a new home and coincidentally was approaching graduation in an MBA program.

Over the past year, the manager recorded the following *positive* events in a critical incident log:

Received a higher-than average merit increase.
Attended creative leadership seminar.
Appointed to profit improvement task force.
Attended training society convention, with spouse, at company's expense.

In addition, the following *negative* events were recorded:

Recommendation for department expansion rejected.
Criticized for spending beyond budget.
Strong disagreement with one of the field sales managers over administration of the training program.
Candidacy for a promotion to the personnel department unsuccessful.
Sharp increase in workload as a result of reassignment of responsibilities.

After analyzing the situation, the manager concluded that Bob would probably change jobs within a year. Naturally, he tried to prolong that period, but at the same time he identified a replacement within the organization and arranged for him to receive accelerated development. Thus when Bob left, about ten months later, the manager was in a position to fill the vacancy immediately with a highly qualified candidate who was "ready" for the assignment.

ASSESSING READINESS FOR PROMOTION

An important part of human resources planning is assessing the readiness of employees for promotion. Some employees may be ready immediately; others may be ready after additional training and development; and the remainder may be nonpromotable.

Managers have a different responsibility toward each of these groups. For employees who are ready now for promotion, the manager should utilize their capabilities by assigning extra responsibility and by searching within the organization for appropriate assignments at a higher level.

For employees who need training and development to become ready for promotion, the manager should create an individualized program designed to strengthen their skills.

For the nonpromotables, the manager should consider ways to add variety and challenge to their current jobs and, if possible, retrain them to qualify for lateral job assignments. Otherwise, the nonpromotables are likely to "turn off" and may search for other employment.

In assessing the promotability of employees, managers should consider the following criteria:

Mental ability.
Energy level.
Desire for advancement.
Capacity for and willingness to assume responsibility.
Interpersonal skills.
Communication skills.
Organization and planning skills.
Tolerance of uncertainty.
Resistance to stress.
Flexibility.
Need for approval of superior and peers.

When an organization operates an assessment center, these criteria can be assessed formally. However, the formal assessment should be a supplement to, not a relacement for, the manager's personal assessment.

In addition to evaluating criteria for promotion, managers should ask themselves these general questions:

Is the employee growing in the job?
If the employee has stopped growing, can I stimulate new growth?
Has the employee outgrown the job?

ORGANIZATION RENEWAL

Human resources planning demands that managers look beyond their own responsibilities. They should learn about the human resources needs of other business units and should advise other units of their own needs. In this way different units can be developing replacements for one another. In one organization, for example, the manager of manufacturing and the manager of marketing have an ideal relationship. Promising manufacturing staff members have received sales force assignments, and sales representatives have been appointed to production staff assignments. Both departments regularly feed each other's needs. The beneficiaries are the organization and the employees.

In addition to developing a pool of replacements within the organization, managers should develop an external pool. It is important that they recruit continually, rather than just when the need arises. By doing so, they develop recruitment sources and locate attractive candidates whom they can call upon when necessary. One of the most effective human resources planners I know regularly talks to two or more potential recruits, maintaining their interest in a future assignment with the organization. One of the by-products of a continual recruitment program is that the manager learns about the changing market value of his or her current employees. It's critical that a manager learn—before employees do—whether they are being paid below market value. The manager can then close the gap between what employees are currently being paid and what they can get at another company.

THE ROLE OF PERSONNEL

Managers often hold polarized views of the role of the personnel department in human resources planning. Some managers feel, "The personnel department should do my human resources planning." Other managers feel, "Personnel doesn't do anything. It can't help me with my planning."

Neither point of view describes the most effective relationship between the manager and personnel. Human resources planning is the manager's responsibility, but the personnel department can offer substantial assistance. Certainly as a source of career information, it can be of value. In serving as an interface between departments, personnel is in an ideal position to help. And in developing an internal and external replacement pool, it performs a valuable function.

Thus managers don't have to "go it alone" in meeting their staffing needs. They should use whatever help they can get to guarantee a steady supply of human resources to minimize turnover.

COMMONSENSE ACTIONS

1. As a manager, you should regularly monitor your unit's workload. A helpful technique for doing so is shown in Figure 24. First, calculate the man-hour capacity

Figure 24. Monitoring workload.

| | Hours | |
	Estimated	Actual
Man-Hour Capacity		
(weekly)*		
Regular hours	375	359†
Acceptable overtime	20	30
Total Capacity	395	389
Forecasted Workload		
Routine projects	240	260
Special projects		
1.	50	65
2.	75	50
3.	45	65
Total Workload	410	440
Gap	15	51

*Staff of 10
†Includes absences

of your unit. For example, a manager of ten people, each working a regular 37½-hour week and willing to work a maximum of two hours of overtime per week on a regular basis, has a total man-hour capacity of 395 hours.

Next, forecast the workload of the group. Estimate the number of hours the group will spend on routine activities. Then estimate the number of hours required to complete special projects. Weekly, compare the estimate for the week with a man-hour audit, according to time sheets. A continuing gap suggests the need for a staff adjustment.

2. Each quarter, review your critical incident log to search for patterns in employees' complaints. When several employees appear to be having similar problems, you or the organization may be creating an unhealthy work environment.

You might summarize the log entries according to these categories:

Work environment problems

Growth problems

Promotion problems

Pay and benefits problems

Work assignment problems

Supervision problems

3. Schedule a formal meeting with other department heads to discuss promotable subordinates. This will give you a forum for sharing data about future staffing needs, for identifying candidates for promotion, and for discussing their development needs.

4. Establish a working relationship with the personnel department. Discuss and negotiate your respective roles in human resources planning. Most important, develop a spirit of mutual cooperation and interdependence.

PART FOUR

RETAINING
VALUED
EMPLOYEES

This part of the book examines preventive maintenance—the measures managers can take to preserve a high-quality workforce and to recognize and retain valued employees who are interested in a job change.

Chapter 18 examines how the exit interview can be of value in "saving" an employee, and in helping a company to learn about problems that could lead to the loss of other employees.

Chapter 19 discusses ways to help employees work through problems that might precipitate a job change, and emphasizes early intervention when employees have reached the turn-off point in their jobs and/or in the organization.

Chapter 20 explores counseling strategies under varying conditions, such as:

o Employee announces intention to leave but is not committed to leaving.

- Employee is bitter about leaving and has ill-will toward the organization.
- Employee leaves with unresolved claims that could lead to a legal battle.
- Employee has been terminated, and the organization would like to offer outplacement.

CHAPTER 18

The Exit Interview

ALTHOUGH the exit interview is becoming more common in organizations, its value is questioned by many managers. The prevailing attitude was expressed to me by one first-line manager:

"I'm not certain if the benefits of exit interviews are greater than the problems they create. Outgoing employees generally whitewash their negative feelings, or they go to the other extreme and describe all sorts of problems that exist only in their heads. I know of several instances when an exit interview led to a witch-hunt that caused serious problems for over a year."

The manager was rightfully concerned. Employees may withhold or color information. Even under the best conditions, when employees leave they may feel emotional about it. They are leaving friends and a familiar environment that has some pleasant memories for them.

Even though employees may be emotional and resist talking freely when they leave, there is much to be learned from holding an exit interview. The departing employee may have many of the same complaints as employees who are staying. The first clue that a serious problem exists may be revealed during an exit interview. For example:

During an exit interview, a highly placed manager in a large health care company revealed that the turn-off point in his job occurred when he was asked to attend a six-month training program at a leading university. Since the organization had invested a considerable amount of money in his education, he assumed that a better work assignment would be waiting for him when he completed his special program. Instead, he went back to his previous work assignment.

Investigating the lead from the exit interview, the interviewer discovered that the same pattern had occurred at least ten times before over a two-year period. In effect, the decision to invest in advanced education for key employees without identifying a better work assignment in which employees' new skills could be used was leading to turnover.

When problems are not attended to during the exit interview, they can explode into trouble. The employee may eventually bring them to court, to the EEOC, or to the Civil Liberties Union. Aggrieved employees want satisfaction. It takes less to satisfy an employee if his problems are properly attended to at the exit interview. If they have not, he may stew over his disaffections for months and then submit unreasonable demands.

Another advantage of the exit interview is that it offers

the company an opportunity to leave the door open for rehiring employees in the future. An employee may assume that he or she can't go back when a new job goes sour or turns out to be less than expected. However, if it is made clear in the exit interview that valued employees are welcome back, they are more likely to give it full consideration. I know of several dramatic examples of employees who were enticed to other organizations only to find out that things weren't as expected. Thereafter, they returned to their original organization, performing outstandingly as stable, valued employees.

MISHANDLING THE EXIT INTERVIEW

The substantial value of the exit interview may never be realized if the interview itself or the findings are mishandled. Here are some common practices that can destroy the value of the exit interview.

Impersonal Yes-or-No Forms

Some organizations that claim they conduct exit interviews in reality administer impersonal questionnaires which limit the employee's response. The employee is kept at arm's length and is not encouraged to talk freely and openly.

This kind of interview is relatively easy to conduct and very safe: both the employee and the interviewer are protected from emotionalism. However, the narrow questions are ineffectual in uncovering the *real* problems associated with turnover. Instead, they require only socially acceptable answers, such as "I am leaving this job for more money," or "I am leaving this job for a better opportunity."

Wrong Interviewer

Employees won't risk sharing their real feelings unless they are confident that the interviewer will handle their responses with care. Often, however, the interview is conducted by a uninterested person from another department who is performing a routine job. Or, worse yet, it may be conducted by someone who the employee feels has an ax to grind.

An employee is more likely to reveal confidential thoughts to someone he or she knows well, respects, and trusts. Carefully selected and trained old-timers can be very effective as interviewers. Also, staff personnel who traditionally work closely with line personnel and have earned their goodwill can perform well as interviewers.

Employees typically describe the most desirable interviewer as follows:

"Before I level with anybody during an exit interview, I want to make sure that he will protect my interests."

"I'm willing to talk to someone who knows me and my work situation well. I want him to consider me as an individual whose opinions and feelings deserve a full hearing. Most important, I want to be treated with respect and consideration."

Wrong Timing

Most exit interviews take place after the official announcement of resignation or termination. By that time, it's virtually impossible to *save* the outgoing employee. It's too late to help the employee rethink the decision and possibly reverse it. Employees are busy thinking about their future and have psychologically withdrawn from the company. Also, during the period before the official announcement, employees are apt to be more spontaneous in expressing their feelings. Thereafter, they will probably "talk out" their feelings with family members and coworkers, and their comments will lose candor.

Plunging In

Interviewers often expect too much too soon from exiting employees. After five or ten minutes of questioning, they want employees to reveal answers to such sensitive questions as:

Did you get along with your boss?
What do you dislike about the company?
Were you treated unfairly?

Very few employees are likely to open up to the interviewer early in the interview. Usually, the interviewer will have to lead them slowly, proceeding from *easy* to *hard* questions. Then the hard questions will have to be approached tentatively and indirectly.

Ignoring Emotions

Usually, the exit interviewer feels uncomfortable with any display of emotion. He will tend to ignore emotion, acting as if it were not present. This may alienate the employee, who will interpret the lack of response as coldness and lack of interest. Typically, the departing employee feels, "This interviewer couldn't care less about me." Rather than ignoring emotions, the interviewer should acknowledge them openly, demonstrating that he is fully tuned in to the exiting employee. A simple declaration like "I see you are really upset" can help to dispel emotion and keep it from blocking the interview relationship.

Overreacting

Departing employees often rationalize their departure by diminishing the value of the organization they are leaving. In effect, they are saying:

"My departure doesn't bother me because there were things about the organization that I didn't like. I may be leaving friends and some good memories, but I'm also leaving some people I didn't like and unpleasant memories."

This process of "putting down the past" to minimize the

sense of loss can color the employee's reported grievances. Thus the exit interviewer must interpret the employee's remarks with care. Initially, he should accept them without question. But as the interview progresses, he should try to explore them in an nonthreatening way. For example: "Earlier you mentioned that other people in the department were also unhappy with the closeness of supervision. Why don't you tell me more about that?"

The interviewer should informally check with other people in the organization to verify some of the "facts" collected in the interview. Only after the investigation confirms what he was told should he present his findings to higher management for possible action.

INVOLUNTARY SEPARATION

When employees are asked to leave the organization involuntarily, the exit interview is likely to be particularly emotional and difficult. Not only are terminated employees suffering from a sense of loss; they are also being rejected, and their self-esteem is under attack. Under these circumstances, it's natural for employees to feel upset and hostile. Regardless of the justification for their dismissal they will tend to blame it, in all or in part, on the organization.

The exit interviewer should not try to defend the company or justify the action it has taken. This will only alienate the employee and negate the value of the interview. Whatever explanation the interviewer could supply, it probably would not satisfy the aggrieved employee.

After searching out the facts, the interviewer should get the employee to shift from lamenting what has happened to preparing for the immediate future. For example, the interviewer might ask: "What are your plans now, and can I help you?" A considerate and thoughtful exit interviewer can help the employee overcome self-defeating anger and redirect his thinking to finding another job. Otherwise, the employee may feel vengeful and may not be satisfied until he can "get back" at the organization.

Thus the exit interview serves many purposes. It can help to identify problems that have led to turnover and that may continue to create turnover. It can provide an opportunity to retain employees who have said they are leaving but have not really committed themselves to leaving. And it can help employees who are bitter about leaving work through their bitterness and redirect their energies to future planning. However, all these benefits are realizable only when the exit interview is properly conducted. Otherwise, it can cause more harm than good.

COMMONSENSE ACTIONS

This chapter has examined areas in which the exit interview is commonly mishandled. A commonsense action is to pay close attention to these pitfalls and to make sure you are conducting the interview properly. You may find it helpful to follow the suggested interview format outlined below.

1. *Statement of purpose.* The employee doesn't know what to expect during an exit interview. He is concerned about the confidentiality of his remarks and possible repercussions. Also, he doesn't know what benefits, if any, there are in talking freely. Therefore, as interviewer, you must establish immediately the kind of protection the employee will be given and the benefits to be gained in talking freely.

2. *Relevant background information.* Ask the employee to describe his main duties and the people with whom he worked regularly. This is a nonthreatening request which orients the interviewer and helps to make the employee feel comfortable talking.

3. *Positive aspects of the job.* Ask the employee to review his major duties and key relationships, and to describe positive aspects of the job. This helps the employee put things into perspective: no matter how unhappy he

currently feels, there are aspects of the job that he has enjoyed.

4. *Negative aspects of the job.* The employee may be hesitant to answer questions about negative aspects of the job. In particular, he may be unwilling to reveal problem relationships. You may have to draw out some of this information, supplying specific leads such as:

"Tell me about the amount of variety in the work."

"How would you describe the workload?"

"How close was the supervision?"

"What did you think of the working conditions?"

5. *Critical incidents.* Try to determine whether anything has happened during the past year or two that has upset the employee or been unresolved. Perhaps there has been a significant change in the way business is conducted in the work unit. Or perhaps changed relationships have created problems.

6. *Reasons for leaving.* After the negative aspects of the job and unresolved grievances have been explored, the employee may feel that he has clearly identified his reasons for leaving the job. However, the real reasons may be totally unrelated to the employee's expressed areas of dissatisfaction. That's why the reasons for leaving should be explored separately at this point in the interview.

7. *Suggested changes.* Even employees who have been close-mouthed about the reasons for their dissatisfaction with the company may make suggestions for change that reveal their real feelings. It's hard to resist the temptation to tell a company how to "do things right."

8. *Separation agreements.* In the final stage of the interview, you should define the terms of the separation, describing what the employee is entitled to and what the organization expects from the employee. If the employee is being terminated, the discussion might also include the kind of help the organization can offer in finding another job. (See Figure 25.)

This interview format is flexible, of course. If an employee talks freely and at length, you may have to ask few

Figure 25. Separation agreement.

Severance pay of \$_____ and the attached description of benefits have been granted pursuant to satisfactory execution of the following responsibilities:

☐ Outstanding assignments completed.
☐ Maintenance reports and records reassigned.
☐ Committee membership reassigned.
☐ Supplier contacts notified.
☐ Customer contacts notified.
☐ Temporary replacements trained.
☐ _____
☐ _____

In addition to carrying out the responsibilities described above, I agree not to malign the company or any of its employees.

_____
Signed (Employee)

questions, except to focus the discussion. If the employee doesn't talk freely, you may want to follow the steps more closely.

The following dialogue demonstrates the sequence of steps in an exit interview:

INTERVIEWER   When an employee leaves the organization, an exit interview is required. In this final discussion, we hope to learn about anything that may have lessened your satisfaction with the organization and that may be affecting employees still with the organization.

EMPLOYEE   I don't gain anything by complaining about past wrongs. Besides, I don't want to leave enemies behind me. I may need a reference some day.

INTERVIEWER   I appreciate your concern about discussing unpleasant issues, particularly if you feel that such a discussion may backfire on you. But I'm sure you

would like to help good friends you are leaving behind. And I personally will guarantee that anything
you tell me will be confidential. (*After stating the purpose of the interview and convincing the employee
that he can help others by being candid, and can do
so with impunity, the interviewer begins to gather relevant background information.*)

INTERVIEWER   Tell me about your job.

EMPLOYEE   What do you want to know?

INTERVIEWER   Your main duties, and the people you
worked with regularly. (*This question helps to orient
the interviewer, and at the same time is a nonthreatening request that gets the employee to start
talking freely.*)

INTERVIEWER   (*After listening to the employee's description*) It certainly sounds as if you had a responsible
job. What aspects of the job did you enjoy the most?

EMPLOYEE   I guess it might sound peculiar for somebody
who just quit to say that I liked most aspects of the
job. I liked working with a lot of different people, I
enjoyed the autonomy, and I really liked calling on
customers. Many of them have become personal
friends. (*No matter how unhappy the employee may
feel at the present time, he can usually recall positive
aspects of the job.*)

INTERVIEWER   Obviously, since you decided to leave the
organization, there must have been some negative aspects of the job too.

EMPLOYEE   Nothing special. (*If the employee is hesitant
to discuss the negative aspects of the job, the interviewer should draw out this information.*)

INTERVIEWER   I'm sure that nothing special was negative.
Nevertheless, I would like to explore some specific
areas. (*The interviewer explores the nature of the work
assignment, the workload, the quality of training,
working conditions, pay and benefits, promotional opportunities, and working relationships. The interviewer accepts whatever the employee says and*

doesn't pass judgment. *Instead, he encourages the employee to explore each statement further by making such neutral comments as "Tell me more," "That's very interesting," and "Can you give me some specifics?")*

INTERVIEWER   What has happened in this last year that you found dissatisfying?

EMPLOYEE   I guess there were a few things that really disturbed me. On top of the list is the fact that I didn't get a promotion that I thought I was directly in line for. Also, my boss gave me a performance rating of "average," and I feel that I performed much above average. In fact, this is the only time in my career that I have ever gotten an average rating. Finally, I have had some serious financial problems, and the 5 percent raise I got didn't do much to alleviate them. *(After exploring the negative aspects of the job and recent critical incidents, the interviewer attempts to relate them to the employee's stated reasons for leaving the organization.)*

INTERVIEWER   You told your supervisor that you were leaving primarily for more money, but I wonder if some of the incidents we've discussed aren't also related to your decision to leave.

EMPLOYEE   I guess you're right. I probably never would have started looking for a job if I wasn't having trouble with my boss. He just hasn't been the same since our department got a new director. The director puts pressure on him, and he's been putting pressure on all of us.

INTERVIEWER   All of us?

EMPLOYEE   I'm not the only one who feels the way I do. There are others in the department who may be staying but not for long. *(The greatest value of an exit interview is that it helps to uncover the pockets of discontent and working conditions that may be a source of dissatisfaction to others.)*

INTERVIEWER   You sound concerned about the welfare of

your fellow employees. What recommendations would you make for improvement?

EMPLOYEE   I'd get rid of the new director.

INTERVIEWER   I'm sure you may feel that he has created many problems for you. But what specific things would you want to change? (*Often disgruntled employees will suggest sweeping changes and may want to attack people who they feel are responsible for their dissatisfaction. In this case, the interviewer should direct the conversation toward recommendations that are practical and reasonable.*)

INTERVIEWER   Whatever you have told me will be given careful consideration. Certainly, you have made some suggestions for change that deserve further investigation. I will bring them to the attention of management.

Now let's consider the terms of your separation. Specifically, I'd like to discuss the provisions that have been made on your behalf and the responsibility of employees when they leave an organization. (*The interviewer defines the terms of separation, describing what the employee is entitled to and what the organization expects from the employee—such as confidentiality of trade secrets, cooperation in the continuity of assignments, and agreement not to disparage or cause harm to the organization.*)

CHAPTER 19

Retention Strategy

WHENEVER you suspect that a valued employee is thinking about leaving the organization, you have to decide what you can do to change the employee's mind. You might ask the employee directly, "Are you planning to leave?" or you might probe indirectly, asking, "How are things going?"

Often the employee will deny that he has any plans to leave. If he admits the truth, he may place his current job in jeopardy, as the company may start looking immediately for a replacement. However, you do not have to confirm that the employee is planning to leave before you take action. If you think your suspicions are well-founded, you can start planning a retention strategy now. An initial step in developing a retention strategy is to clarify your reasons for wanting to retain an employee. Ask yourself these five questions:

1. *Do I want to retain the employee for business or personal reasons?* Perhaps the employee is a likable person who is easy to manage yet may be only a mediocre performer.

2. *Am I dependent on the employee, and if she leaves will it hurt me?* You may be holding on to the employee even though it is not in the best interest of either the employee or the company to keep her in your department. Perhaps she would be willing to stay if she were transferred to another department.

3. *Do I want to retain the employee just to avoid short-term problems?* You may not have the time or inclination to recruit a replacement, and the workload may be so heavy that you feel you would rather retain a mediocre performer than face a vacancy.

4. *Am I afraid I might be embarrassed if the employee leaves?* You may feel that to some extent you are responsible for the employee leaving, and you are concerned that others would become aware of it. The resignation would not make you look good.

5. *Do I feel it is politically necessary to retain the employee?* Maybe the employee is in a "protected" category (minority, older worker), has many friends in the organization, or has been with the company for years. You feel that if you do not retain the employee, even though the decision to leave was voluntary, others will feel that you did not try hard enough.

If your answers to these questions indicate that you are motivated to retain the employee for personal rather than sound business reasons, you should probably not intervene. Instead, allow the employee to leave the organization. Regardless of how sensitive management may be to turnover statistics, it's unlikely that the company would want to retain employees who are not genuinely valued.

Assuming that you decide an employee is worth retaining for sound business reasons, you next have to make some general strategic decisions.

STRATEGIC DECISIONS

One of the first things you must decide is, "How much time do I have to change the employee's mind?" If you are fortunate enough to recognize the employee's dissatisfaction early, when thoughts about leaving are just beginning to emerge, you can act without a sense of urgency, since you may have months to influence the employee. On the other hand, if the employee has had feelings about leaving for some time and has been active in the job market, you may have only weeks or days to act.

Another general decision you must make is, "What is my trading stock?" In deciding what enticements might help you retain the employee, you should define your negotiation limits in writing so you know in advance what concessions you might offer (compensation, special assignments, training, job redesign, benefits, and so on).

If you do not define your negotiation limits, you may *overpromise* in your discussions with the employee, or you may reach the point of convincing the employee to stay and then be unable to agree on some mutually acceptable action. Instead, you may be forced to say, "I'll have to check with my boss and get back to you."

Another important decision you must make is, "Would temporary retention be acceptable?" Over the long run an employee will probably leave. Nevertheless, in the interest of the organization and the employee, it may make sense to try to prolong the employee's stay for another year or two. Perhaps by then a suitable replacement can be found and trained or arrangements can be made for a redistribution of workload. Also, during that period the services of a highly valued employee will be available to the organization.

CAUSES OF RETENTION STRATEGY FAILURE

There are valuable lessons to be learned about retention strategy from examining the causes of its failure. Many commonly used strategies just don't work.

A highly popular strategy is *persuasion*. A manager tries to talk an employee into staying, relying on words and emotional appeals to friendship or loyalty. The problem with this strategy is that it may work for a very short time—but then the employee is faced with exactly the same unresolved problems.

Another strategy is *tokenism*. The manager tries to retain the employee by making immediate token concessions and promising more in the future. The employee may stay, only to find that the future promises are not lived up to. As a result, the employee feels deceived.

Whitewashing is a common strategy when a manager learns that an employee has been talking to search firms or actively interviewing for a new position. The manager encourages the employee to confide in him and seek his counsel on suitable new employment. He says, "I certainly don't want to lose you. But if you're intent on leaving, keep me informed about the opportunities so that I can give you the benefit of my knowledge of competitive companies." Then, as each opportunity is presented, the manager explains why it is completely "unsuitable."

Another strategic ploy is *weeping*. The manager spins a poignant tale of the amount of grief and pain he and other members of the work group will suffer when the employee leaves. Such an appeal to the employee's sympathy may create feelings of guilt and may delay her, but it is unlikely to retain her indefinitely.

A final retention strategy that often backfires is *intimidation*. The manager attempts to frighten the employee, citing the dangers of going to a strange organization and leaving the known for the unknown. Like all the other strategies, this approach is rarely effective because it does not address the employee's concerns or the issues that led to the decision to leave.

RECOGNIZING EMPLOYEES' SELF-INTERESTS

The success of any retention strategy depends on emphasizing the employee's needs and wants rather than the organization's. The employee's interests are paramount in his mind when he is contemplating leaving an organization. Let's consider some employee interests that are often not given full consideration when developing a retention strategy.

Advancement

It's natural for employees to be concerned about their "rate of advancement" in the organization. If their career stalls for too long a time, the chances of moving it upward again begin to diminish. The longer someone stays in a job, the more he or she is identified with that activity and judged to be unqualified for higher-level assignments requiring different skills.

When employees feel blocked or "typed," it is difficult to convince them otherwise. Instead, the manager should accept an employee's feelings and develop alternative courses of action that are compatible with these feelings. For example, if an employee feels that she has been typed, the manager may offer to vary her work assignment so that she can prove to others that she has capabilities beyond those she has demonstrated in the past.

Type of Work

When an employee feels that a work assignment is not challenging, he will resist any attempt to convince him that it is "not as bad" as he thinks. He wants and needs more work variety. An appropriate retention strategy here is to add variety to the employee's work assignment or, perhaps, transfer the employee to another assignment in the organization.

Conflict

When an employee is embroiled in conflict, she may seek relief from the daily pain it causes by leaving the organization. A retention strategy based on such appeals as "Don't let it get to you" and "Are you going to let them drive you out of the company?" offers no relief to an employee who is feeling pain. Instead, the manager should help the employee resolve the conflict or at least try to soften its impact on the employee.

Missteps

As an employee's career matures in an organization, he may accumulate black marks on his record and may acquire detractors. Eventually, he may reach the point where he feels the organization is no longer the right place for him. A retention strategy that attempts to "prove" him wrong is doomed to failure. Instead, an appropriate strategy is to focus on joint problem solving to reduce the urgency and seriousness of the employee's feelings.

Mistreatment

When employees feel that they have been mistreated, rational arguments probably won't change their minds. Employees not only want to right the wrong; they want retribution. Their attitude is, "You hurt me and now I want to hurt you back."

In this situation, an appropriate retention strategy is to acknowledge the employee's "hurt" and to take steps to prevent a recurrence of the same kind of mistreatment. Most important, you should offer at least a mild form of retribution to provide satisfaction to the employee. For example, the employee's manager might receive an official letter of rebuke. Or the employee might receive a retroactive adjustment in compensation.

EXAMINING YOUR OWN ATTITUDES

In developing a retention strategy, you should examine your own attitudes, making certain that you can answer the following questions with an emphatic yes:

- Am I trying to satisfy mutual needs and wants?
- Am I setting a precedent that I can afford to follow in the future?
- Am I making promises that I can deliver?
- Am I excluding personal issues such as loyalty and friendship from my retention strategy?
- Am I accepting the employee's feelings as legitimate, and as a starting point for problem solving?

SUCCESS STORIES

Retention strategies that address an employee's self-interests can work even when the employee is determined to leave the organization, as the following case histories attest.

For over ten years Abe was a field sales manager for a leading pharmaceuticals company, responsible for a region of 150 sales representatives. However, personal problems began to compromise his work performance, and he considered leaving the organization. The national sales manager's retention strategy was to help Abe cope with his personal problems by reducing the amount of work pressure on him. Thus the national manager encouraged Abe to stay with the company in a lesser capacity, as a sales representative. In the three years since his demotion, Abe has resolved his personal difficulties and has performed well as a sales representative. It is highly likely that he will be given a field management assignment again, and he is confident that he will be able to handle it now that his home life has stabilized.

In order to add challenge and variety to her work life, Ellen planned to accept a job in another organization. She was highly regarded by co-workers and was extremely important to the organization because of her very specialized capabilities. Ellen was certain that she would be stuck in the same assignment indefinitely.

Recognizing Ellen's feelings, her supervisor identified transfer opportunities for her and suggested that she stay in the organization but join another department. Ellen gladly accepted a transfer, because she liked the organization and really didn't want to leave. She has proved to be just as valuable in the new work assignment, and even though her former supervisor had to replace her, at least he saved her services for the organization.

Les was the only old-timer in a department made up primarily of young and inexperienced employees. He decided to leave the organization because he no longer felt comfortable in the department and was somewhat resentful that his career had stalled, even though he realized that he had probably reached his level of competence.

His supervisor acknowledged Les's feelings directly. He suggested that they jointly develop a plan that would allow Les to spend more time with co-workers closer to his own age and, at the same time, give him the feeling that he was performing in a capacity that somebody with his years of service deserved. Accordingly, his job was redesigned so that he could spend a greater amount of time working on interdepartmental team activities, such as a cost improvement project and a work simplification program.

Les stayed, and over the last five years he has contributed substantially as a member of these interdepartmental teams. Also, as the younger people in his department became more experienced, and as Les got to know them better, he was able to improve his working relations with them.

Obviously retention strategies that start with an employee's self-interests are much more successful than those that depend on manipulation and that have the organization's interests primarily in mind.

COMMONSENSE ACTIONS

Six steps can help you develop an effective strategy for retaining employees.

1. *Early recognition.* Whenever you observe any changes in an employee's attitude or behavior that suggest dissatisfaction, assume the employee may be considering changing jobs. Don't ignore the many warning signals of an employee's discontent. Whatever retention strategy you develop, it has a much better chance of working when you see the employee early, before he is fully committed to leaving the organization.

2. *Attention.* Once you recognize that an employee is a candidate for resignation, schedule an interview to explore his wants and needs. Give him your full attention and hear him out. Don't offer premature advice or make any effort to resolve his problems. Instead, just find out what's bothering him.

3. *Identification of the source of the employee's problem.* Find out where the problem lies: Is something wrong at work, or at home? Is something wrong in the department, or in the organization? Is something wrong with what the employee is doing now, or with the overall work assignment?

The purpose of identifying the source of the employee's dissatisfaction is to determine whether the problem is within your control. If it is, you can bring about changes directly. If it is outside your control, you may be able to help the employee explore alternative courses of action.

4. *Selection of retention strategy.* Remember, any retention strategy starts with a recognition of the employee's

needs and wants and gives full attention to the employee's feelings. The strategy should either change conditions that are troubling the employee or help the employee work through his feelings so that he can better live with conditions as they are. And the changes should be arrived at through *mutual* problem solving.

5. *Follow-through.* After you agree on the conditions under which the employee would be willing to stay, you have to follow through to make sure things happen as promised.

6. *Feedback.* Meet regularly with the employee to make certain that the original sources of dissatisfaction have been resolved and that other problems have not developed. Old wounds don't fully heal. Sometimes, relatively minor events can reopen them.

The following dialogue illustrates an interview between a supervisor and an employee who may be planning to leave the organization.

SUPERVISOR   I've had the feeling lately that you have something on your mind.

EMPLOYEE   Why do you say that?

SUPERVISOR   Well, you appear to be preoccupied and much more reserved than you usually are. (*An employee may not admit that she has decided to leave the organization and has been looking for a job, but after sufficient probing she is likely to acknowledge that she has had some problems.*)

EMPLOYEE   Yes, I'm a little upset.

SUPERVISOR   Tell me more about it.

EMPLOYEE   There's not much to tell. I just haven't had very good work assignments.

SUPERVISOR   You feel that I have given you worse assignments than other people in the department?

EMPLOYEE   I don't know if you've done it deliberately, but I haven't had very good assignments.

SUPERVISOR   Which assignments didn't you like? (*The supervisor hears out the employee's complaints, accepts whatever the employee says, and listens without evaluation.*)

SUPERVISOR So you feel that you are burdened with an excessive amount of paperwork which you consider to be drudgery, and that you haven't had an opportunity to visit the field and interact with customers as frequently as you would like.

EMPLOYEE Yes, that's correct.

SUPERVISOR (*The supervisor attempts to gain agreement on the problems that are disturbing the employee.*) I value your services, and I know that you won't stay in my department, or with this organization, unless we can resolve these problems.

EMPLOYEE I don't know whether I would leave or not, but I certainly am unhappy about what's been happening to me.

SUPERVISOR Do you have any suggestions on what we might do to resolve this problem? (*The supervisor encourages the employee to participate in problem solving, trying to guide her toward a mutually satisfying solution.*)

SUPERVISOR So I may be able to reduce your paperwork load somewhat and increase the number of field trips you make, but I probably can't *completely* satisfy your wishes. Can you live with the changes I am proposing?

EMPLOYEE I'm not sure. I have a feeling that another job might satisfy my needs more completely.

SUPERVISOR That may be true. But have you thought about what you would give up by leaving? (*The supervisor helps the employee consider all aspects of the decision to leave. Often, the employee sees only the obvious benefits and doesn't fully appreciate some of the disadvantages. Of course, the supervisor must be careful not to get into a debate, with the employee arguing why she should leave and the supervisor arguing why she should stay.*)

SUPERVISOR I'm pleased that we have worked out some changes that make you feel better about your job. I'd like to meet with you again next month, after we've set these changes in motion, to see how things are working out. In the meantime, if anything happens that you'd like to talk about, please come into my office any time. (*Even though a satisfactory solution appears to have been arrived at, the supervisor schedules a follow-up interview and encourages continuing feedback.*)

An essential part of any retention strategy is to pay close attention to employees during the period that they are deciding whether to leave or stay, and during the period when a proposed solution is being implemented. Thereafter, periodic checks should be made to determine whether there has been any change in the employees' feelings.

CHAPTER 20

Counseling Leavers

WHEN an employee is leaving an organization, the manager who assumes responsibility for counseling the employee is faced with a dilemma: he has two clients, the departing employee and the organization, and often these two clients have conflicting objectives.

Frequently the conflict is resolved in favor of the organization. And counselors become primarily organization advocates. However, by not meeting their obligation to employees, the counselors may hurt *both* the employees and the organization.

Every separation involves some bad feelings. Certainly, employees who have been terminated or laid off are usually somewhat resentful and hostile. Even employees who have resigned were probably dissatisfied before they considered changing jobs. Counselors are in a unique position to provide needed assistance to such employees and at the same time to gain substantial benefits for the organization. They can profoundly affect the employees' *aftertaste*—their lingering feelings about the organization—and can minimize future problems resulting from bad feelings.

Counseling Objectives

A primary reason employees develop a bad aftertaste is that during the last phase of their employment they received virtually no counseling, or inept counseling, from their managers. Typically, the managers do not realize what can be accomplished in the critical phasing-out period and do not set clear counseling objectives.

In counseling involuntary leavers, the following objectives apply:

1. *Minimize bad feelings.* Unless the counselor succeeds in minimizing the bitterness and resentment that an employee feels, the organization may face continuing disputes and legal claims after the employee leaves. And since the employee usually maintains relationships with friends in the organization, he may influence their feelings about the company.

2. *Assist in adaptation.* The departing employee needs to make both short-term and long-term adjustments. Immediately, he will be concerned about providing himself and his family with a continuation of income and benefits. Thereafter, he will need to find an appropriate job as soon as possible.

3. *Offer constructive criticism.* An employee may continue to repeat the same mistakes and fail in job after job because she has never been told specifically why she has failed. While the counselor should not force the employee to listen to a painful rehash of her past failures, he should advise her of the strengths on which she can build a future career and the weaknesses that may cause her future problems.

4. *Preserve self-esteem.* The employee hasn't failed as a person; he has failed in a job assignment. An important counseling objective is to help the employee feel good about himself, regardless of the reasons for termination.

5. *Leave a lifeline.* Organizations usually sever all ties with employees who are terminated—even employees who have had long and faithful service. The counselor should demonstrate that his personal interest and the organization's interest in the employee extend beyond current employment. Certainly, the company is interested in the employee's future well-being.

In counseling voluntary leavers, a different set of objectives applies:

1. *Create a "friendly" competitor.* Voluntary leavers often join competitive companies. If they leave under completely friendly terms, they're less likely to "pirate" or engage in other acts of retaliation against a past employer.

2. *Develop a source of referrals.* An employee who leaves an organization under friendly terms can be a good source of referrals. He may direct business to his former company or suggest that qualified people seek employment there. In effect, he can serve as a valuable goodwill ambassador.

3. *Rehire.* The counselor should make it clear that the door is open for valued employees to return. Some employees may learn shortly after leaving that the new job is not what they expected. Even an employee who has been gone from the organization for several years, acquiring valuable new skills, may want to rejoin the organization in a higher-level capacity.

4. *Reassign duties.* Although an employee may be committed to leaving a particular department, she might be willing to stay with the organization, accepting responsibility in another department. If a reassignment isn't immediately available, the manager might arrange for the employee to work on temporary special projects. He might encourage the employee to initiate contacts with other department managers to seek a future reassignment.

5. *Negotiate to retain valued employees.* When employees resign, they are not necessarily committed to leaving. In fact, they find it painful to leave. The counselor may be able to negotiate relatively minor concessions and successfully retain the services of valued employees.

Counseling Guidelines

There are several important guidelines that the counselor should follow in counseling involuntary and voluntary leavers. These guidelines can help the counselor achieve his objectives and avoid problems.

1. *Involuntary leavers.* Always allow terminated employees to vent their emotions. Until emotions are released they will stand in the way of counseling.

When acting as counselors, many managers are intimidated by employees' emotions and react defensively. They themselves become emotional and try to argue employees out of their feelings. ("You shouldn't feel that way. The company and I have always been very fair to you. You have no right to get upset with us.") Instead the counselor should accept the employee's feelings—without agreeing that the company is guilty of any wrongs.

After the emotions subside, the counselor should shift the discussion to problem solving and future plans. ("Let's talk about your future. How can I help you while you are finding a suitable new job?")

Finally, the counselor should determine whether the employee feels better as a result of the interview. Some key questions that can help to determine the impact of the interview are:

How do you feel about what we discussed?
Do you feel confident about the future?
What are your feelings about the organization now?
How do you feel about yourself?

2. *Voluntary leavers.* Don't assume that voluntary leavers are truly committed to leaving the organization. Often, to relieve the painful should-I-leave-or-should-I-stay conflict, employees make an arbitrary decision to leave. Then

they glorify the advantages of the new job, convincing themselves and others that it was the right decision.

The seemingly confident employee who announces enthusiastically her decision to take another job really has many doubts. The counselor should try to uncover those doubts by getting the employee to talk freely about her feelings.

Remember, counseling is not advice giving. For the first half hour of the interview, the counselor should do little talking. Instead, he should attend to what the employee says and respond primarily with verbal acknowledgments and checks for understanding. In addition, the counselor may initiate a few broad leads:

Tell me about your new job.

What do you think will be the main problems you'll be facing in your new job?

When the counselor is convinced that the employee is well informed about the new job and has realistic expectations, he can determine whether the employee has made a sound decision. If the decision appears to be unsound, the counselor can reinforce the employee's natural doubts and try to negotiate an agreement to stay. The counselor may be able to make immediate changes that will remove the employee's reasons for leaving. Or he may be able to set in motion actions that will eventually alleviate the employee's complaints.

If meaningful changes can't be made, and the new job represents a genuine opportunity for the employee, the counselor should focus on building goodwill and leaving the door open in the event the new job assignment doesn't work out.

Benefits of Effective Counseling

The following case histories attest to the value of effective counseling.

Barbara was the only female branch manager in a large organization. Her high energy, drive, and ambition contributed to her success—and also created many interpersonal problems. for her. Because of her impressive record, she was wooed by other organizations and eventually accepted an attractive offer from one of them.

When her manager met with her to discuss her resignation, she talked continually for half an hour, volunteering comments about what was wrong with the organization and praising her new employer. The manager patiently listened to what she was saying, responding minimally and neutrally. After a while Barbara became repetitive, and the emotional tone of her conversation quieted. Recognizing the change in tone, the manager began to review Barbara's points, testing the level of her conviction: "You said that a female branch manager doesn't have the same amount of authority in this company as her male counterpart. Is that one of the major reasons you were receptive to a job offer?"

As the manager reviewed her points, Barbara began to qualify some of her statements and put them in perspective. By the conclusion of the discussion, both Barbara and her manager realized that it was not necessary for her to leave to satisfy her primary desires. The fact that she had been appointed branch manager was convincing evidence that women could move up. She began to see that the only real barrier to her future progress was her inability to get along well with others. Most important, Barbara recognized that the interpersonal difficulties she was having at this company would probably follow her to the other company unless she changed her work style.

Barbara decided to stay, telling her manager, "I don't know if I'll be successful in mending the fences I knocked down, but I owe it to myself to try."

Arnold was an assistant purchasing agent in a medium-size organization for 27 years. During this period, his performance was acceptable but not outstanding. When the organization was faced with economic setbacks, Arnold was terminated.

At the counseling interview, Arnold appeared reluctant to talk, but his distress was evident. Arnold's manager wisely selected a subject that Arnold would be willing to talk about—separation pay and plans for continuation of benefits.

The conversation progressed logically to Arnold's future job plans. Although he was very concerned about his future, he hadn't taken any action, because he wasn't really sure how to search for new employment. The manager explained the outplacement services available and in the process made it clear to Arnold that the organization was interested in his well-being and was prepared to give him outplacement assistance.

By the end of the interview, Arnold recognized that his termination had resulted from extraordinary economic conditions. He was still unhappy about it, but was far less resentful and bitter.

The progress the counselor had made during the interview was summed up by Arnold's concluding remarks: "I certainly don't like what happened to me after 27 years of service, but I realize now it was a business decision, and you would not have fired me under ordinary circumstances."

Thus effective counseling benefits both the employee and the organization.

COMMONSENSE ACTIONS

1. Counseling is not a naturally acquired skill. Line managers need training, particularly in listening and responding. An effective training method is to use videotaped models depicting appropriate counseling styles in different situations.

2. The organization, through its human resources department, should issue an official policy on counseling objectives. Every manager should know definitely if the organization encourages rehiring, transfers, and so on.

3. Issue a policy on negotiation terms: the concessions that can be made to retain potential leavers. In trying to retain employees, managers may promise more than they can deliver. Or they may be reluctant to make any concessions because they are uncertain about what the organization will allow.

4. The organization should supply outplacement assistance for involuntary leavers. This can range from modest support services, such as typing, mailing, and telephone answering, to retaining outside services.

5. The counselor should prepare a separation review, describing the outgoing employee's responsibilities. (See Figure 25.)

PART FIVE

COMMONSENSE INTERPERSONAL SKILLS

Throughout this book I've stressed the line manager's responsibility to confront turnover, often by initiating one-to-one dialogues with subordinates. However, to be able to do so requires interpersonal skills. This part of the book sets forth a number of guidelines for improving interpersonal skills.

Chapter 21 discusses how to challenge subordinates who are acting in a nonproductive way. Chapter 22 examines how harsh discipline can destroy productivity and morale. It can help managers systematically review their own disciplinary practices and learn how to discipline more intelligently.

Chapter 23 analyzes bad communication habits and offers advice on how to overcome them. Chapter 24 explains how to look a problem square in the eye, analyze it, recognize your part in it, and change your ways accordingly. Finally, Chapter 25 reviews the role of the manager in helping employees solve personal problems that are affecting their performance at work.

CHAPTER 21

Constructive Confrontation

IT IS easy to function well in a harmonious work environment, where things go smoothly and everybody is cooperative and agreeable. But in the real world, things frequently go wrong, and the people you work with become uncooperative and disagreeable. Functioning well in this kind of environment takes considerable skill.

Particularly important is the ability to challenge subordinates who are acting in a nonproductive way. You want to make them examine their behavior and its consequences more carefully. This invaluable skill is called *confrontation*.

While its potential to improve a situation is great, confrontation is a tricky skill to master, since it can backfire easily and degenerate into accusatory name calling. Even so, it is a necessary part of your repertoire of managerial techniques. It helps you build stronger relationships with others by increasing the quality of your involvement with them. It leads to a deeper understanding and a clearing of the air. It also protects your self-esteem, since it lets you stand up for your rights and express your feelings.

Confrontation can be useful in several kinds of situations. We'll touch on five of the most common.

1. *When you want to correct a misunderstanding.* Perhaps somebody disagrees with you because he doesn't have all the facts or has been misinformed. In this case, you must confront the employee and set him right. Let's look at an example: Two employees in your department have been acting very cool and aloof ever since you told them about a change in the work schedule. You suspect they have been misinformed about the schedule change and decide to confront them.

"Something seems to be bothering you, and it upsets me too," you begin. "Ever since I changed the schedule, our relationship has been deteriorating. What's the problem?"

One employee replies, "Can you blame us? We have seniority and can't see why we should have to work every other Saturday."

"Before you became supervisor," the other employee joins in, "seniority had certain privileges around here."

The air starts to clear now as you explain, "I agree that seniority should have privileges, but I had no choice in this case. Let me tell you why we had to change the schedule."

2. *When you want to encourage action.* Perhaps one of your staff members is dragging her feet on a project or not meeting your expectations in some other way. To get her to change, you might try this confrontation:

"Julie, I'd like to review your productivity with you. I don't know whether you realize it or not, but your performance is about 25 percent below the department standard. Let's see if we can find out what is keeping you from meeting the standard."

3. *When you want to uncover hidden strengths.* Many people work below their capacity. Often they do so because they either don't recognize or underestimate their own abilities. By confronting these underachievers, you may help them realize their unused strengths.

Here's a typical example: Whenever a special problem develops, one knowledgeable but insecure employee runs to his supervisor to "check things out." The supervisor is concerned about this behavior because it wastes her time and inhibits the employee's growth. She decides to confront the employee:

"Jim, almost every time you refer a problem to me, I get the feeling that you already have a good idea of how to handle it. What do you think?"

4. *When you want to correct a weakness.* This is a very common type of confrontation and a particularly unpleasant one. Because few people take criticism well, correcting a weakness is much harder to do than uncovering a hidden strength. It is, nevertheless, a necessary and legitimate confrontation, and one that must be handled tactfully. You might adopt an approach like this:

"Helen, I got three reports this month of discrepancies in the reports you're responsible for. Let's discuss them and determine how to avoid them in the future."

5. *When you want to overcome experiential differences.* Few people see things exactly alike all or even part of the time. Differences in perceptions, feelings, or values can contribute to distortions and misunderstandings. Or people may deliberately try to mislead you by playing games or not being completely on the level. In these cases, a confrontation can be helpful in reconciling the differences:

"Mary, I'm concerned about the way you respond to my requests."
"But I always do what you tell me," Mary replies.

"Yes, I know you do. But you seem to do it reluctantly, and I'd like to țry to solve this problem."

She breathes a sigh of relief and says, "Since you brought it up, let me say that I've been very unhappy because I feel I've been forced to take on a much heavier workload than anyone else in the department."

CONFRONTATION GUIDELINES

To handle these confrontations more effectively, you might follow the guidelines described below.

Preconfrontation Planning

As mentioned earlier, confrontation carries certain risks. Before you attempt it, you should plan carefully. Ask yourself the following questions:

- Why am I planning the confrontation? Do I really want to increase understanding with the other person, or do I have some other motive? Is this an authentic issue, or am I manufacturing it?
- How good is my relationship with the person I am confronting? Is he likely to feel that I truly have his concerns at heart?
- Is this a good time or a bad time for a confrontation? Is the other person under any unusual pressures that might interfere with the success of our talk?
- Are there any constraints that might keep the other person from responding?
- If he acts on my requests, will it create a hardship for him?

Here is an example of how preconfrontation works:

A supervisor has had longstanding problems with his director; as a result, their relationship has been strictly business. Recently, the director has made unusual work demands on the supervisor. The supervisor recognizes that recent vacancies have created the problem, but even so he thinks the demands are excessive and wants to confront the director to get an accumulation of grievances off his chest.

After reviewing the list of preconfrontation questions, however, the supervisor decides not to do it at this point. He realizes that the timing of the confrontation is not right, because the director has been under unusual pressure. Since his relationship with the director has always been relatively poor, a confrontation now would probably be unsuccessful.

The Confrontation

Perhaps the best advice anyone can give you about attempting a confrontation is to proceed with caution. Instead of plunging in, approach it tentatively, feeling your way and continually checking on the effect you're having. Here's an example of how to have a productive confrontation:

A purchasing agent wanted to confront a manager on his method of ordering supplies. The manager often wrote orders hurriedly, and his handwriting was almost illegible. But instead of telling him to be more careful, the purchasing agent explained that some of his personnel were having trouble interpreting the orders. The manager responded with the suggestion that purchasing supply preprinted forms to avoid the problem in the future. Thus a confrontation produced mutual understanding and paved the way to solving the problem.

In any confrontation, you should always focus on the here-and-now. It's unproductive to dredge up something from the past. To be relevant and effective, a confrontation should deal with current issues. Remember, too, to focus on the *behavior* that you find undesirable. Don't attack the other person. Be specific and factual, avoiding any attempt to interpret why the other person acted as he did.

Don't, for example, say: "Your failure to complete assignments indicates that you have little interest in your job."

Try this instead: "Your assignments for July 15, 22, and 27 were all incomplete. Tell me what the problem was, and we'll talk about how to keep it from happening again."

Find your target the same way an artilleryman finds his. He fires a salvo and watches where it lands. He then adjusts his sights to get closer to the target and with successive salvos zeros in on the target. This method is called successive approximation. Each statement you make should move you closer to your goal. When you make a point, wait for a reaction—either verbal or nonverbal—to determine how to phrase your next statement.

Suppose, for example, that you have a troublemaker in your group. She is continually getting into arguments with the rest of the staff. You want to confront her on this issue without getting involved in an unproductive argument, so you try successive approximation:

"I understand that you and Fran had another argument yesterday."

"It wasn't my fault," the employee replies. "She's always trying to pass her work off on me."

You readjust your sights and fire again: "It may not have been your fault, but this is the fourth argument you've had in the last month."

"That's true," she admits, "but I don't know why it happens. I don't try to provoke anyone."

Now you're getting somewhere. You try to sound sympathetic, but at the same time, you let her know you want to solve the problem: "I'm sure you don't provoke people. But I'm concerned about the effect these arguments are having on the department. Maybe you're doing something you're not aware of that sets them off."

Effects of the Confrontation

In order for confrontation to be effective, you must adjust your approach according to the impact it has on the other person. If the other person summarily denies or rejects what you say, you're missing the target and must try a different approach. If the other person counterattacks and tries to discredit you or what you've said, you're off-target again. Sometimes, it may appear that you have been completely successful with your confrontation because the other person seems to accept everything you said. But in fact he may be agreeing with you simply to get you off his back. When you suspect this is happening, keep checking your perceptions to make sure that the other person isn't just feigning agreement.

In other cases, an employee may ignore the confrontation by acting as though she didn't hear what you said. Perhaps she finds criticism intolerable and chooses not to hear it. Or she may accept your comments selectively, hearing only what she wants to hear and distorting any negative remarks.

By monitoring the effects of your confrontation, you can see what you have accomplished and plan what to do next.

Remember, confrontation takes skill, and it can backfire when done poorly. But despite the dangers involved, confrontation is vital to a healthy working relationship. Without it, unresolved issues constantly get in the way. By confronting them, you can remove them permanently and strengthen a relationship.

CHAPTER 22

Creating the Right Disciplinary Climate

AN UNCOMPROMISING disciplinarian is a destructive supervisor who demoralizes and alienates his staff. He doesn't ask, he tells. The uncompromising supervisor overpowers her subordinates, giving them no leeway. She uses discipline like a club.

Why do some supervisors believe in strong discipline? Often they are unconsciously mimicking their parents' treatment of them: their parents may have been harsh and uncompromising. Or they may be following the example of a past supervisor whom they respected. Perhaps they have some compelling personal needs, such as:

- A need to control because the supervisor fears being controlled himself.

- A need for status. Harsh discipline is the supervisor's way of showing that he's the boss.
- A fear of failure. She's tough on her staff because she doesn't want to displease her own manager.
- A need to be perfect. A perfectionist keeps making new demands on himself and his staff.
- A need to be insulated. He doesn't want any backtalk, so he bullies his staff into silence.
- A lack of self-confidence. She uses discipline to keep her staff at a distance so they won't be exposed to her uncertainties.
- A need to feel important. By putting down others, she increases her own self-esteem.

One of the consequences of uncompromising discipline is frustration for both the manager and his staff. The manager will be frustrated because no matter how hard he leans on his employees, some of them will fight back. And they'll grow hostile and defensive, arguing with him overtly and defying him covertly. Others will escape to other jobs or become involved in outside activities. The staff will be frustrated because no matter what they do, they won't be able to please their boss.

Reactions like the following are commonplace in departments with harsh disciplinarians for supervisors:

"I dread every time my boss works with me because he keeps finding things wrong. When I'm with him, I feel as though I have two left feet. The way he rides me, I get the feeling I'm the worst technologist in the world, even though I've always done well."

Another inevitable consequence of unyielding discipline is poor performance. Subordinates grow fearful working under a harsh supervisor. They are afraid to act on their own initiative and become uninspired conformists. Their thinking is routine, and they are preoccupied with safety and orderliness. They do only what they think will please the supervisor and lose interest in all other goals.

Even when a supervisor learns the serious consequences

of keeping the reins too tight, she may find it difficult to change her style. Then other problems can develop. For example, the supervisor may go out of her way to avoid conflict, and as a result the group may suffer from lack of discipline.

When people do things they know are wrong, they expect punishment. If the punishment isn't forthcoming, they may try to see how much they can get away with. If the supervisor fails to react to any of the infractions, they may think she's afraid to.

A manager must choose a middle ground between too much discipline and too little. And before he can do that, he must abandon the idea that punishment is a win-lose game—that either he wins and the others lose, or they win and he loses. When discipline is handled intelligently, neither the supervisor nor the staff loses. Instead, they all abandon practices that are hurting the company, themselves, and their futures.

Intelligent disciplinarians set reasonable boundaries, leaving plenty of operating room but clearly designating off-limits areas. The boundaries should be wide enough to allow for mistakes that will not cause irreparable harm but will help employees establish their own limits. The ideal disciplinary climate is one in which the staff can learn *self-discipline*. Here are two examples:

A normally productive and responsible employee who was preoccupied with marital problems made a series of mistakes. When her supervisor discovered the mistakes, he was tempted to criticize her sharply. But he realized it was the first time this problem had occurred and that the employee's past record was spotless. Instead of calling her in and lecturing her, he brought the errors to her attention and asked her to take steps to avoid another occurrence.

Shortly afterward the employee, who had been troubled by the episode, brought the subject up herself. This is how her supervisor responded:

"I'm sure those errors worried you a lot. It's obvious that you recognized their seriousness and that you knew we couldn't tolerate their recurrence. I'm confident you won't let them happen again."

A hardworking employee neglected her routine reports, even after her supervisor reminded her to be more diligent. Instead of censuring her and demanding an explanation, the supervisor reviewed his expectations with the employee. He told her he expected everyone to complete routine reports carefully. Then he asked her to recommend a fair schedule of discipline for future noncompliance. Both he and the employee confirmed the agreed-on policy in writing.

The supervisor thus avoided lecturing the employee on her past behavior and imposing disciplinary measures that had never been discussed. His objective was not to punish, but to avoid future undesirable behavior—and the strategy worked.

Even when a supervisor creates an almost ideal climate for self-discipline, someone will cross into restricted territory. Often the reason is that the employee has different standards from the supervisor. He doesn't think he's doing anything wrong.

Say, for example, that the supervisor wants an employee to start work precisely at 9:00 A.M. and finish at 5:00 P.M. The employee feels that as long as he puts in an eight-hour day, it makes no difference if he comes in late and leaves late. What he's overlooking, of course, is the effect his behavior has on everyone else's work—and morale.

GUIDELINES FOR HANDLING DISCIPLINARY PROBLEMS

Disciplinary problems are inevitable. As a manager you should regularly review your disciplinary practices. The quiz in Figure 26 can help you do that systematically.

Figure 26. How do you score as a disciplinarian?

Yes	No	
		I *Preparation for the Disciplinary Session* 1. Did you pick the right time and place? 2. Did you set the stage? 3. Did you depressurize? 4. Did you state the issues impersonally? 5. Did you project the possible consequences?
		II *Search for the Root of the Problem* 1. Did you find out what started the trouble? 2. Did you find out what sustained the trouble? 3. Did you search for feelings related to the facts? 4. Did you uncover the unmentionables? 5. Did you identify differences in goals, needs, and points of view?
		III *The Disciplinary Session* 1. Did you encourage the employee to do most of the talking? 2. Did you stay in character? 3. Did you avoid getting trapped in the employee's problem? 4. Did you suggest alternatives? 5. Were you kinder than expected?
		IV *Self-Analysis* 1. Did you listen? 2. Were you impartial? 3. Were you credible? 4. Did you guard against ego satisfaction? 5. Did you avoid becoming emotional?

Score five points for each "yes," and deduct five points for each "no."

100–90   You are an excellent disciplinarian.

89–80   You are a good disciplinarian; try harder to upgrade yourself to "excellent."

Under 80   You are a poor disciplinarian. Unless you learn new disciplinary methods and change your methods, you will alienate employees.

Think back to your last confrontation, take the test, and record your score. After completing the quiz, consider the following points and let them be your guidelines in the future.

Preparation for the Disciplinary Session

1. Pick the right time and place. The best time to discuss discipline is as soon as you see the problem developing. Choose a place where you will have complete privacy and preferably where you can block out interruptions and phone calls. The environment should let you both feel comfortable. Don't put the other person in a chair facing your desk. Instead, pull two chairs together and sit facing the employee without any barriers between you.

2. Set the stage. Explain what the problem is and what facts you have gathered. Present the facts in a rational, nonaccusatory manner.

3. Depressurize. If the employee gets emotional in response to the fact, don't proceed until he has had a chance to discharge his emotions. One of the best ways to do that is just to sit silently and let him talk.

4. State the issues impersonally. Don't put a personal twist on the facts. Treat them as though neither you nor the employee were involved in the situation you are discussing.

5. Project the possible consequences. The best time to think about the consequences is at the very beginning of the session. If you recognize the consequences of mishandling the situation, you're more apt to be patient and look for ways to solve a problem without seriously hurting either yourself or the employee.

Search for the Root of the Problem

1. What started the trouble? Look for the single event that touched off the problem. Don't waste time on subsequent events that aren't the gut issue—even though they may have made the problem more severe. If the source of

the trouble can be identified, it can be solved. That's why it's so important to pinpoint it.

2. What sustained the trouble? Sometimes the original cause of a mistake no longer exists, but the problem lingers on. Why?

3. Look for feelings related to facts. By merely evaluating the dry facts, you may conclude that the employee is irresponsible. But when you understand his feelings, you may realize that what he did was logical in his own mind.

4. Dig out the unmentionables—those important facts that the employee won't divulge unless you draw him out. He may be embarrassed to admit them, or he may feel they're things you don't tell your supervisor. But knowing them is often essential in solving the problem.

5. Identify differences in goals, needs, and points of view. Is the employee deliberately misbehaving, or does he just disagree with what he's being asked to do? Or are the company's standards and practices contrary to his personal goals?

Disciplinary Session

1. Encourage the employee to do most of the talking. The best way to discipline is to let the other person talk. Only then will the true reasons for misconduct be revealed.

2. Stay in character. If you're normally tough, don't soft-pedal your feelings. You'll lose credibility. On the other hand, if you're normally soft-spoken and controlled, don't try to impress the employee with a theatrical display of anger.

3. Don't get trapped in the employee's problem. Sometimes an employee is so convincing in explaining his reasons for misconduct that you start sympathizing with him and end up condoning his action—even though it violated rules that are fair and important.

4. Suggest alternatives. When an employee's wrong actions are based on a sincere difference of opinion, try to find a compromise that he can come to terms with.

5. Be kinder than expected. A subordinate is more likely to accept disciplinary action if it's not as harsh as he expected. He should leave your office with a sigh of relief, knowing that you tried to correct, not punish.

Self-Analysis

1. Be sure to listen. Listening means not only hearing what was said but empathizing with the other person and reading between the lines.

2. Be impartial. If other staff members were in the same situation, would you treat them the same way?

3. Be credible. Does the employee believe what you say? A supervisor sometimes shouts and threatens during a disciplinary session, but the employee knows the supervisor doesn't really mean what he's saying.

4. Guard against ego satisfaction. If you go into a disciplinary session to get revenge, to punish, to blame, or to satisfy some other personal need, you're only feeding your ego. The same is true if the employee goes into the session motivated by pride or a need to show off.

5. Don't get emotional. You won't accomplish anything, and you may even make things worse if you lose control. Intelligent discipline is firm and fair, and allows room for human error. As a supervisor, you must remember that disciplinary problems can arise from reasonable sources: sincere differences in goals and standards, disagreements over current policies and procedures, and extraordinary situations that lead employees to step out of bounds.

Systematically review your own disciplinary practices and the guidelines discussed here. Above all, try to create a climate for self-discipline. If you do that, you'll have far fewer problems.

CHAPTER 23

Correcting Communication Faults

MOST supervisors don't think about how effective their communication is. They assume they're getting through to others. But they rarely check to find out for sure.

A supervisor who communicates ineffectively may know what he's talking about, but nobody else does. Whenever he writes or talks to others, he confuses them. When other people try to explain things to him, he hears only what he wants to hear. He leaves a trail of misunderstanding behind him.

COMMON COMMUNICATION FAULTS

Underlying fuzzy communication are several common faults. (See Figure 27.)

Figure 27. Common communication faults.

A supervisor who is guilty of . . .	Has this weakness . . .
Not thinking things out	Delivers half-developed ideas
Lack of understanding	Misinterprets and distorts others' meanings
Disorganization	Continually changes the subject
Fear of communication	Makes blandly inoffensive and confusing statements
Poor delivery	Talks down, lectures, and irritates
Lack of consideration for others' needs and drives	Thinks "I" instead of "you"
Overcrowded communications	Treats important information as an afterthought.
Overreliance on the grapevine	Creates an information famine.
Failure to listen	Doesn't give employees a full hearing

1. *Not thinking things out.* Often a supervisor doesn't take the time to think things out. And under these circumstances he delivers a jumble of half-developed ideas.

2. *Lack of understanding.* When a supervisor doesn't fully understand, she's often embarrassed to ask for more information. Instead, she interprets as best she can, distorting the speaker's or writer's intended meaning.

3. *Disorganization.* Disorganization may be the result of fuzzy thinking or of inexperience in communicating. Whatever the cause, it's hard on listeners. A disorganized supervisor says one thing, jumps to something else, then returns to the original subject, and may even go off on another tangent before he's through. Trying to keep up with him is like riding a merry-go-round.

4. *Fear of communicating.* Sometimes a supervisor doesn't want to upset his staff members and is afraid of repercussions. Yet he feels duty-bound to follow his boss's instructions and passes them on in the least offensive way. He succeeds only in confusing everyone.

5. *Poor delivery.* Without realizing it, a supervisor may turn off her listeners by her manner or tone of voice. Perhaps she talks down to them or lectures them. As a result, her staff members get only halfway through her memos before tossing them into the wastebasket. Or they simply stop listening while she babbles.

6. *No consideration for others.* Anyone who is totally self-absorbed is an ineffective communicator. The me-first type tells others what to do; he doesn't ask them what they want to do. His sentences almost always start with "I."

7. *Overcrowded communication.* At the other end of the spectrum is the supervisor who wants to create a good-guy image. He's so busy sharing the latest gossip, discussing sports, or just relating some recent experience that he delivers important information only as an afterthought.

8. *Overreliance on the grapevine.* Often a supervisor knows she communicates poorly, so she doesn't do it at all. Members of her staff suffer from an information famine. The grapevine flourishes in this atmosphere, with employees passing secondhand and thirdhand information back and forth. Everything grows increasingly muddled and inaccurate.

9. *Failure to listen.* With many supervisors, the inability to communicate clearly is only half the problem. The other half is a failure to listen to what is being said. I once asked a group of employees what made it difficult for them to communicate with their supervisors. Here are some of the responses:

"Our supervisor insulates herself from us. When she asks for something, it's only because she wants to confirm her preconceived ideas. She screens out anything contrary to her own point of view."

"My supervisor won't listen to the facts. He gets emotional at the drop of a hat and shouts down what I have to day."

"We get into arguments about things that can't be proved. I'll say one thing, and she'll say another. Neither of us has any evidence. We just ping-pong words back and forth."

"He has his mind made up when we start to talk. Before I can tell my side of the story, he has already decided whether to accept or reject it."

"When I send my supervisor a memo of more than one page, she won't read it. She wants everything presented simply. Unfortunately, a lot of my problems aren't simple."

"My boss doesn't show any respect for me. He doesn't pay attention when I am talking to him. He interrupts before I am through, and he's easily distracted. He doesn't care about my point of view."

COMMUNICATION CHECKLIST

Using the communication checklist shown in Figure 28, you can test your effectiveness as a communicator. Let's take a closer look-at the items listed.

Facts
To avoid confusion and misunderstanding, you should make an effort to gather pertinent facts, hearing the other person's side of the story. Ask yourself whether the facts are consistent and logically related—that is, whether one naturally follows the other.

By carefully gathering the facts, you can avoid many common communication faults.

Feelings
Facts are only part, and sometimes a small part, of any communication. It's critical that you try to determine how

Figure 28. Communication checklist.

1. *Facts*
   □ Do I have all the pertinent facts?
   □ Are the facts consistent?
   □ Are the facts logically related?

2. *Feelings*
   □ How high is the level of feelings (SUDS level)?
   □ Have underlying feelings been identified?
   □ Are feelings distorting perceptions of the facts?
   □ Are feelings contradictory to the expressed facts?

3. *Points of View*
   □ Do we understand each other's point of view?
   □ Are our points of view founded on accurately perceived facts?
   □ Is our behavior consistent with our respective points of view?

4. *Needs*
   □ Have I identified the underlying needs?
   □ Can I satisfy the other person's needs as well as my own?
   □ Have I established priorities for our needs?

high a level of feelings—both yours and the other person's—is involved.

Pay particular attention to whether the other person's nonverbal cues are consistent with what he is saying. He might say, for example, "The extra workload doesn't bother me at all." But the expression on his face is really saying, "I am terribly upset about the extra workload."

Psychological researchers track the emotional content of personal events in terms of *subjective units of discomfort* (SUDS). Someone with a high SUDS level is generally agitated and upset; someone with a low SUDS level is calm and relaxed. In any communication situation, you should determine whether the person you are dealing with has a high, medium, or low SUDS level. High feelings tend to distort a person's perception of the facts. And a SUDS level that is contradictory to the facts indicates that some hidden considerations haven't yet come to the surface.

Feelings are particularly important in evaluating the amount of trust involved in the situation. Distrust interferes with accurate communication. People rarely make direct statements like "I don't trust you or what you're saying." But their feelings are revealed nonverbally, particularly in the form of increased tension.

Points of View

True communication isn't possible until the people involved understand each other's point of view. Once understanding exists, it's possible to decide whether both points of view are based on an accurate perception of the facts. Misunderstandings and conflict can often be resolved this way. And it can also help explain what may have appeared to be irrational behavior.

Needs

Communication isn't complete until it is understood, accepted, and acted upon. Acceptance and action are based on satisfaction of personal needs. In any communication situation, you have to ask yourself, "Am I satisfying my needs and those of the other person? Are our needs mutually exclusive?" Since it will probably be impossible to satisfy all your needs, it's important to set priorities. Then you can address those needs you feel are most important.

The following example shows how the communication checklist works.

Not long ago, Tom Foley, a veteran employee, complained to his supervisor, Shirley Atkins, about what he felt was an unfair performance rating. Here's what he said:

"I'm hardworking and conscientious. I haven't had one sick day all year. I'm never late. And you never see me taking long coffeebreaks. I can't understand how you could give me a below-average rating."

Shirley agrees that Tom is a conscientious worker and she mentally starts to review the checklist. She realizes that she doesn't have all the facts of the situation and will have to establish them. So she asks Tom to comment on the quality of his work.

This is obviously a sensitive area for Tom. His SUDS level rises, his face gets red, and his facial muscles tense. He stammers, "I—I do a good job. I'm one of the most experienced technologists in the laboratory."

Shirley nods and says, "You're a highly experienced employee. Maybe that's why I expect you to adhere to high standards and work with minimum supervision."

This makes Tom admit that his error rate has increased over the past year and that he hasn't been showing enough initiative, often preferring to dump his problems on his supervisor.

When he makes these admissions, Tom's SUDS level drops—and this surprises Shirley. It doesn't seem to bother him at all to discuss his shortcomings. But whenever he refers to the appraisal, he grows much more emotional. This prompts Shirley to probe the next item on the checklist: feelings.

"You seem very upset whenever you talk about your performance rating," she remarks.

"Of course, I'm upset," he responds. "I don't think it's fair."

Instead of defending herself against Tom's accusation, Shirley tries to draw him out. She wants to understand his feelings, which appear to be distorting his perception of the facts. She finally hits paydirt when she repeats something Tom alluded to in one of his remarks.

"I get the idea that you think other people in the department are getting better performance ratings than they deserve."

"Right." Tom agrees vehemently. "A lot of people make mistakes and get away with it. I never do."

"It sounds as if you think I have a double standard in appraising people in the department. I can understand why that would upset you."

Shirley knows that she is communicating well, because at this point Tom beams and his SUDS level drops. She moves on to the third item on the checklist: establishing both points of view.

"Tom, let me see if I can describe how we both feel about this situation. You don't dispute the facts on which the appraisal is based, but you do feel that I have a double standard, demanding more of you than of others in the department. For my part, I think I've tried to judge you according to the facts, taking into consideration that you have 20 years of experience and are capable of top performance."

Tom agrees that this is a fair statement of the situation. Shirley then proceeds to the fourth checklist item: satisfaction of needs.

"I would love to be able to upgrade your appraisal rating. Let's discuss how we can both walk away from this discussion more satisfied."

In the discussion that followed, Tom recognized that it wasn't unreasonable for Shirley to expect more from him than from less experienced people. But he also revealed his strong need for attention. Because Shirley spent less time supervising him, he felt ignored. He needed regular encouragement and acknowledgment of his contribution. Recognizing this strong need, Shirley developed an improvement program based on closer interactions with Tom.

By the end of the discussion, Shirley made it clear that she appreciated Tom's abilities, and Tom promised to upgrade his performance. Thus real communication took place between the two. They understood each other, and Tom accepted and promised to act upon Shirley's suggestions.

As you can see, the checklist serves as a systematic guide to help uncover facts, feelings, points of view, and needs. It helps you diagnose specific communication problems. By clarifying troublespots through self-analysis and continual probing, you will strengthen your communication skills. The rewards for your effort will be more accurate and more productive communication.

CHAPTER 24

Recognizing Problems— and Your Role in Causing Them

WHEN things go haywire, many supervisors are guilty of two nonproductive and often destructive activities. The first is trying to sidestep direct responsibility for foulups. Remarks like "It wasn't my fault!" and "We didn't do anything wrong!" are common from sidesteppers. The second tactic is looking for someone else to take the blame. "That's the other department's job, not mine!" and "You rushed me!" are common excuses from blamers.

The following scenario in a hospital laboratory shows these techniques at work:

The pathologist was on the warpath. He had just received several calls from clinicians who were complaining about late reports. Smarting from these attacks, he stormed into the chief tech's office and demanded an explanation.

The pathologist was less interested in correcting the situation than in venting his emotions and giving the chief tech a thorough dressing-down. He had been embarrassed, and he wanted to make someone else pay for putting him in that position.

The chain reaction continued, involving section chiefs, technologists, and technicians—a long trail of sidestepping and blaming. At the end of it all, no one really knew what had gone wrong, but everybody was upset.

Such faultfinding is always counterproductive. When you criticize people, they feel attacked and must therefore defend themselves. The more vigorously you attack, the more persistently they defend. This pattern produces strained relationships and rarely leads to problem solving, which should be your primary focus.

RECOGNIZING THE PROBLEM

To recognize developing and potential problems requires a systematic approach. The questionnaire in Figure 29 offers the supervisor a method for dealing with a problem when it first rears its head. Let's review the 10 key questions shown and see how a supervisor with lots of reports completes the form.

o *What's happening?* Remember that your perception of the truth of the situation may be entirely different from someone else's. Thus, in the hospital example, the pathologist's explanation for a series of late reports may be an unusually heavy workload, aggravated by a vacancy and a summer vacation schedule. But the physicians, who are concerned about their patients' test results, see only that lab reports are taking twice as long as they used to.

Figure 29. Recognizing the problem.

1. What's happening?

As I see it

The workload has been unusually heavy, and it's aggravated by a vacancy and the summer vacation schedule.

As others see it

Lab reports have been late, and lab personnel are becoming increasingly inefficient.

2. Who's involved or likely to get involved?

The original complaint came from several staff physicians. There's a strong probability that other people will get involved — both inside and outside the lab.

3. Have I ever dealt with a similar problem?

Yes, it's a recurring problem.

4. How long has the problem been building?

Since John left — about a month ago.

5. How hot is the problem?

Very hot — the pathologist is furious.

6. Will it get worse if I don't do something now?

Yes, work is backing up fast.

7. How have I contributed to the problem?

I didn't do anything about it earlier.

8. What happens if I can't solve it?

It could hurt my chances of moving up.

9. How much time do I have to solve it?

We should show some improvement in 10 days and should reach a permanent solution in 60 days.

10. What trade-offs am I willing to make?

I can authorize some overtime, and will have to speed up our hiring program.

And they naturally attribute the delay to inefficiency. Obviously, there are perceptual differences here that must be clarified.

○ *Who's involved or likely to get involved?* You may think a disagreement is limited to you and one other person. But other people may become involved. They'll watch developments with interest and may jump into the fracas at any time. In the hospital example, the original complaint was from staff physicians, and it was addressed to the pathologist. But the chief technologist and others soon became involved.

○ *Have I ever dealt with a similar problem?* When the same problem recurs, it's a good indication that you mishandled it the first time. But you can learn from your mistakes. Try to remember which techniques produced the desired results and which ones didn't.

○ *How long has the problem been building?* A developing problem probably hasn't done irreversible damage, but it's important to isolate it before it spreads.

○ *How hot is the problem?* In a typical work situation, there's a fair amount of harmless griping, so you have to be selective about the problems you try to solve. You must determine how much trouble is brewing. If the problem is hot, things could get out of control fast.

○ *Will it get worse if I don't do something now?* It sometimes pays to delay taking action and watch developments. The situation may improve by itself, or you may decide that you can give more time to the problem in the future. In many cases, however, the problem will demand immediate attention.

○ *How have I contributed to the problem?* It makes sense to acknowledge your contribution to the problem. Fooling yourself will only cause trouble. If you're at fault, you can easily solve the problem if you just stop what you've been doing wrong.

In the hospital example, the pathologist should have done something as soon as the vacancy in his department occurred. The already heavy workload and the start of a summer vacation schedule only compounded the problem.

○ *What happens if I can't solve it?* Assess the consequences of failing to solve the problem. Just knowing what you stand to lose may help you find a solution.

○ *How much time do I have to solve it?* Solving a problem too late is just as bad as not solving it at all. If you're dealing with a hot problem, you may have to clear your schedule and concentrate on it alone. In some cases, you may even have to call for outside help.

○ *What trade-offs am I willing to make?* If the consequences of not solving a problem are serious, it pays to make some real concessions in exchange for progress toward a solution.

ANALYZING YOUR ROLE IN THE PROBLEM

After studying a problem, you may begin to suspect that shortcomings in your own supervisory style have demotivated or even estranged your staff. At that point, you should make an effort to analyze your role in the problem. It's difficult, of course, to accept your own faults, and self-analysis is always painful. The questionnaire in Figure 30 can help you analyze your shortcomings objectively.

○ *How would your staff members describe you?* List your positive traits in one column and your negative traits in another. In the second column, you'll find the source of your troubles. In the first column, you'll find ways to overcome them. In the example shown in Figure 30, the supervisor admits that he may not be the easiest person to work with. But by recognizing that he's touchy, unyielding, and hard to approach, he takes the first step toward overcoming some of these negative traits.

○ *Do you treat staff members preferentially?* Like most of us, you naturally like some people more than others and tend to favor those you like. But if your preferences interfere with your fairness as a supervisor, you'll demoti-

Figure 30. Analyzing your role in the problem.

1. How would your staff members describe you?

   Positive

   fair, honest, energetic dependable

   Negative

   Touchy, unyielding unapproachable

2. Do you treat staff members preferentially?

   I give those I trust more latitude, particularly the old pros.

3. How do your own attitudes affect the way you treat your staff?

   I'm not not very tolerant of people—usually younger ones who seem to take their jobs lightly

4. Have you been consistent in your actions, or have you changed recently?

   I've come down harder lately on our new, young technologists.

5. How flexible are you in adapting to the needs of your staff?

   I find it difficult to change my plans.

6. How do you use your authority?

   I tend to suppress complaints.

7. How much independence do you allow?

   Not much. I set narrow limits for independent action.

8. What have you done to build trust and good will?

   When I make a promise, I keep it, and my appraisals are fair.

9. Do you act different under pressure?

   I tend to become more rigid.

10. How must you change?

    I should ease up on my staff, particularly the young people. I should respond more openly to complaints.

vate those who feel they aren't being treated equitably. In the example in Figure 30, the supervisor recognizes that he favors older staff members and therefore has to be particularly careful in dealing with younger employees.

○ *How do your own attitudes affect the way you treat your staff?* Spend a few hours at home in an easychair thinking about why you act as you do. You'll be surprised how helpful this exercise can be. In our example, the supervisor realized that his strong work ethic made him intolerant of young people who appeared to take their jobs lightly.

○ *Have you been consistent in your actions, or have you changed recently?* If you're dealing with a long-term problem, you may find that some of your actions have had a cumulative effect on your staff. If you're dealing with a problem of recent origin, you may be doing something differently that has upset employees. In the example, the supervisor had been exceptionally hard on a new, popular employee. Other members of the staff felt he was riding the employee unnecessarily.

○ *How flexible are you in adapting to the needs of your staff?* Your relationships with staff members are continually changing. Unless you adapt to these changes, it could mean trouble.

○ *How do you use your authority?* Some supervisors suppress employee dissatisfaction by pulling rank when staff members disagree with them. Others fail to exert authority, even when they should. By being sensitive to the way your staff reacts to you, you can find out if you're using authority properly.

○ *How much independence do you allow?* Some supervisors are extremely effective with new staff members who are dependent on them, but they are intolerant of experienced pros who have gained confidence in themselves and want to express their individuality. The supervisor who wants to keep people under his thumb will alienate them. That can be disastrous, because mature, experienced employees are at peak performance levels. In our example, the supervisor recognized that his heavy-handed style would not be well accepted by older, independent employees.

○ *What have you done to build trust and goodwill?* The question is not what you have done *lately* for your staff members, but what you've done all along. An employee may overlook isolated instances of unfair treatment if you have generally been interested in helping her satisfy her needs.

○ *Do you act differently under pressure?* You may enjoy a deserved reputation as an understanding and fair supervisor. But that reputation may have been earned during good times. When a situation goes sour through no fault of your own, does your supervisory style change? People are intolerant of a Dr. Jekyll–Mr. Hyde supervisor. They want and expect consistency. The supervisor in our example tends to become overbearing under pressure. Recognizing this shortcoming, he knows he must take special care to avoid transferring his own stress to the rest of his staff.

○ *How must you change?* Some supervisors believe that they can't change, that they're too set in their ways. But they're wrong! They can change—and they have to change as much as necessary to perform well. Otherwise, their self-made problems will destroy their careers.

COMMONSENSE ACTIONS

1. Strive for early recognition of a problem to help clear up a messy situation. Sidestepping and faultfinding will only make the situation worse.

2. Analyze the problem to determine your role in creating and maintaining it. Improving a bad situation starts with improving the way you handle it.

CHAPTER 25

Helping an Employee Work Through a Problem

SOMEDAY a subordinate may walk into your office and say, "I've got a problem. Do you have some time to talk about it?" But it's not too likely. Generally problems don't come to your attention until they affect an employee's work performance. Marital trouble, for example, may become apparent in the form of absenteeism, tardiness, and careless work.

While you do not have the right to interfere with an employee's personal problems—and shouldn't even want to— the unacceptable work behavior *is* your concern. And you must confront the employee and discuss it. Dealing with the work problem alone and not the total problem takes skill.

Below is a systematic approach for both new and experienced supervisors.

Describe the Unacceptable Behavior

Find out whether the employee realizes that her personal problems have spilled over into the job. You should do this directly, describing the unacceptable behavior in an objective way:

"Nancy, I'm concerned about your recent attendance record. You've been late for work six times in the last two months, and you've been absent an average of one workday a month."

Depending on the closeness of her relationship with you and her willingness to disclose personal information, Nancy may or may not risk sharing her problem with you. She may get defensive and try to deny or rationalize her unacceptable behavior.

Delineate the Boundaries of the Problem

Focus on work performance and not on the underlying personal problem. If the employee offers an explanation related to her personal problem, you should redirect the discussion to the work aspects of the problem:

"Nancy, I am truly sorry to hear that you are having problems with your marriage. I know how upsetting that can be. But that is a personal problem that I'm reluctant to interfere with. On the other hand, your work performance is something that involves me, and something we should talk about."

Agree on the Problem

Once you have established the boundaries of the problem, explore the employee's feelings about it. Find out if the unacceptable behavior bothers her and if she really wants to change. She may feel that you should be making special concessions while she is undergoing such extraordinary personal stress. Until she stops making excuses and agrees that the problem is worth correcting, you aren't likely to resolve it permanently.

Solve the Problem Together

When the two of you agree that a problem exists and must be corrected, you can proceed to working out a solution. Encourage the employee to analyze the situation. Impress on her that you think she can solve the work problem and that you would like to help her try. This will lighten her already heavy load of personal problems.

You might say: "I don't want to bother you now. You have enough on your mind. That's why I want you to improve your work record and get rid of this particular headache. I know you can find a way to come to work regularly and on time regardless of what's happening at home. And I'll support you any way I can."

Your promise of assistance should not be an empty one. This step must really involve *mutual* problem solving. Ask yourself: "How can I make it easier for Nancy to change? How can I show her that I know how hard it is for her to cope with her problem and that I'm willing to be flexible?"

To help Nancy in this situation, you might say: "You said you're too upset to think about work when you've had a fight with your husband. You might find that it helps to come to work even earlier than usual, and I'll try to give you some routine job until you're feeling better."

"You mean to get my mind off my problem?"

"Yes. I'm sure it doesn't help to keep thinking about it. That just makes it worse. I know you enjoy your work, and doing something routine may help you get your mind off your troubles."

"Thanks, I'd really appreciate that."

With this approach, you don't solve the employee's problems, but you make it easier for her to solve them herself.

Reinforce Acceptable Behavior

No matter how good the plan for solving the problem or how strong the employee's intention to follow it, the success of the plan depends on proper reinforcement. When Nancy's behavior is acceptable, be sure to reinforce it, and when it's unacceptable, be certain that you don't reinforce it.

For example, you might suggest: "On days when you feel that you can't possibly get to work yet somehow manage to do it, I'll give you some time to meet with Helen Wilson or a member of her staff. She's the head of the personnel department and has had a lot of experience dealing with families undergoing stress."

"I'd like that. I've met Helen, and I think I could talk to her."

"Let's see how this works for a month or so. At the end of the month, we'll see how you are doing."

Troubled employees usually seek out confidants during the workday to discuss their problems. A supervisor who recognizes this need provides the time "officially" to reinforce acceptable behavior and helps the employee control the amount of time spent talking about personal concerns at work.

Monitor Compliance

In addition to reinforcing acceptable behavior, you should make Nancy more aware of her unacceptable behavior by asking her to keep her own attendance record. Nancy knows that her record will be reviewed at the end of the month, and she'll have to face the consequences of her actions.

Initially, Nancy came to work late or stayed home because she gained by doing so. Her poor attendance record didn't cause her any difficulties at work. In effect, her unacceptable behavior was being reinforced. Under the plan for change, Nancy will get positive reinforcement for coming to work on time and negative reactions—her supervisor's express dissatisfaction—for poor attendance.

Follow Through

The final step is to follow through with the plan and modify it if necessary. Say that at the end of the month Nancy has improved her record somewhat but is still not perfect. In that case, you can further shape Nancy's behavior in the right direction by working with her to set realistic goals and helping her achieve them. For example:

"I really appreciate your efforts. You've been in every day, and you've cut your tardiness in half. You've shown both me and yourself that you can cope with your problems and still get to work on time.

"So this coming month, why not tell yourself that you're going to let yourself be controlled by your emotions only once? If you do that, maybe by the next month you can keep your personal problems completely in check so that they no longer spill over into your work."

This expression of understanding gives Nancy additional time to work out her problems and at the same time suggests a way to eliminate unacceptable behavior.

You may feel that the process described here is too time-consuming and indirect. You may think it is better to issue an ultimatum to shape up or ship out. That's certainly more direct, and in some cases it may work. But it's much more likely to backfire. When an employee is wrapped up in a highly emotional personal problem, he or she finds it hard to think clearly. The prospect of losing a job pales in comparison with the personal problem. Additional pressure from the supervisor, coupled with an apparent indifference to the problem, may actually make the employer's performance worse.

In the course of a career, everybody is challenged by personal problems—health, family, finances, and the like. As a supervisor, it's your obligation to be supportive when an employee is challenged by such problems, but you should not yield to the temptation to share the burden of the problem with the employee.

Instead, you should concern yourself only with correcting the unacceptable work performance. By carefully separating work and personal problems and making it easier for the employee to resolve the work problem, you can help restore good performance.

PART SIX

THE FUTURE

The final chapter in the book, "Emerging Retention Problems," examines recent social changes and the impact they have on turnover. These changes include:

- The rising educational level of the workforce.
- Working couples.
- The changing occupational role of women.
- Second careers.
- The extended retirement age.
- Changes in attitude about the quality of work life.

CHAPTER 26

Emerging Retention Problems

LOOMING in the future are social trends that have the potential to add substantially to turnover. Right now, in varying degrees, they are beginning to have an impact on some organizations. In the future, they have the potential to have strong impact on many organizations.

Let's take a close look at each trend, exploring its dimensions and considering commonsense actions to cope with the problems it poses.

INCREASING EDUCATIONAL LEVEL OF THE WORK-FORCE

The workforce is becoming better and better educated. In an age of technology, well-educated employees are needed. And educated employees want to work in desirable jobs that make maximum use of their education. However, in an economy that is slowing down, the total number of *desirable* jobs cannot keep pace with the number of new, qualified members of the workforce. As a result, competition for these jobs becomes intense, and many employees become frustrated because they are unable to find the positions that they have spent years in college preparing for. People with advanced degrees are forced to take entry-level jobs in fields unrelated to their education, and college graduates with liberal arts degrees are forced to accept *anything* they can get.

Not surprisingly, employees who accept jobs which they feel they are overqualified for and which are unrelated to their interests and education soon become dissatisfied. As a result, they initiate a continual search for the *right* job that takes them from one short-term job to another in rapid succession.

COMMONSENSE ACTIONS

1. In the future, the burden of selection will be even heavier on line managers' shoulders than it has been in the past. Managers are going to have to determine the extent of a job applicant's interest in an open position, and the applicant's willingness to stay with the work assignment for a reasonable period of time. Managers will also have to seek answers to two very critical questions every time they interview a candidate:

- In what ways do you feel the job you are applying for is right for you?
- What role does this job play in your career plans?

2. Assuming that the right candidates have been hired, managers will have to devise ways to extend the employees' tenure beyond the point where they might normally get restless. Managers need to develop challenging special assignments that make the routine more bearable. And they must be willing to accept, and perhaps even advo-

cate, job rotation to give restless employees a change of pace.

WORKING COUPLES

When both members of a working couple are employed at jobs they value, actively pursuing individual careers, conflicts commonly occur. The pursuit of one career compromises the other, creating a problem for the couple and for their respective organizations. The dimensions of this problem were expressed succinctly by a talented woman manager:

"I've worked ten years to get to the point where my organization has offered me the controllership in one of our plants. Ordinarily, I would be jumping up and down with joy. But I don't know if I will be able to accept the promotion. My husband is a tenured assistant professor in a prominent university, and he can't just resign his job and get an equally attractive university appointment elsewhere."

Even when both members of the working couple are willing to relocate, and one of them is not deeply committed to his or her job, the inconvenience and financial burden of relocation create adjustment problems.

COMMONSENSE ACTIONS

1. Provide *total* relocation assistance, financial and general, to the working couple. Unless both members of the couple make a smooth transition, the work performance of the member employed by your organization may suffer.

2. Develop a network of cooperating organizations to provide opportunities for the member of a working couple who is forced to initiate a job search.

3. Maintain current information on the mobility status of a working couple. In this way, rather than forcing a

couple to face an unresolvable conflict, you can help design a career path that won't be disrupting.

CHANGING OCCUPATIONAL ROLE OF WOMEN

Women are moving up in management and will continue to do so in the future. This adds to the problem, discussed earlier, of intense competition for the more desirable jobs. The competition may well become a male/female issue. You may have already heard disgruntled employees explaining their dissatisfaction in sexist terms:

"She only got that job because she's a woman."
"How can they possibly give that job to a man?"

Also, whenever women managers leave their careers to start a family, the work commitment of other women managers is called into question. This can be a continuing source of dissatisfaction and friction, and can lead to turnover.

COMMONSENSE ACTION

No manager can afford to stereotype employees. Every manager should accept responsibility for not allowing work issues to deteriorate into issues of sexual differences.

SECOND CAREERS

As the economy slows, more and more employees find their careers stalling by the time they reach middle management. A growing number of these managers—and even managers whose careers have not stalled—have discovered that the best escape route is to start a second career.

Perhaps, a specialist will decide he can sell his services as a consultant. Or an employee with an enjoyable avocation, such as collecting antiques, turns it into a profitable vocation. Possibly, an employee takes advantage of company-sponsored education to retrain herself for a second career.

Whatever the reason for entering a second career, the impact on the organization is the same: valued employees with long experience leave the workforce.

COMMONSENSE ACTIONS

1. Second-career turnover is most costly when it comes as a complete surprise: management fails to develop an appropriate replacement because the long-term employee is considered "permanent."

To minimize such surprises, encourage second-career counseling and outplacement services. Invite restless employees to discuss future plans, and offer them assistance in making a transition from one career to another. In obtaining such assistance, the employee may discover that his plans are unrealistic or not as attractive as he thought. In addition, you and the employee may be able to find a suitable second career within the organization.

2. A second career is advisable for some employees and can benefit the organization. An employee who has lost interest in her current specialty and is determined to enter a second career loses productivity in her current assignment. It's costly to retain employees whose productivity is declining, particularly when their departure would create promotional opportunities for other valued employees.

EXTENDED RETIREMENT AGE

The extension of the retirement age beyond 65 provides an organization with more productive years from older employees, but it also creates problems that can lead to turnover. Retirements open up opportunities for promotion. Delayed retirements reduce opportunities.

Younger employees often resent elderly co-workers whose energy level and skills may have declined and whose way of thinking may have become outmoded. Many younger employees feel frustrated waiting for somebody to retire who they think will "work forever." Typical of their feelings is this comment from a manager in his mid-thirties:

> "I work for a man who is in his late sixties. He has already had a full work career. I feel it is unfair for him to continue to hold a job that he's been in for so many years. A younger manager with a fresh point of view and a greater energy level ought to be given a chance."

COMMONSENSE ACTIONS

1. The role of older employees should be reexamined. The knowledge and experience they have accumulated certainly should be utilized. However, this does not necessarily mean they should remain in the same jobs they've had for years. Perhaps they should step aside from a work assignment but remain in the organization. They could use their training and experience to help develop the skills of younger managers or to serve as troubleshooters and inside consultants. They could participate as members of project teams.

2. After retraining, senior employees may be able to enter second careers within the organization. For example, an engineer in his sixties with strong interpersonal skills stepped aside from his engineering assignment to take on a recruiting job in the employee relations department. He performed extremely well in the new assignment and served as proof to potential recruits that his organization offered an opportunity for a full career.

QUALITY OF WORK LIFE

For many employees, work is a less important consideration than it has been in the past. Employees work shorter hours and participate increasingly in leisure activities. In addition, more and more employees are demanding jobs that are enjoyable and satisfying. They expect to perform meaningful work and to be treated respectfully by employers.

This new breed of employee is harder to retain. Traditional incentives such as money and promotion have less effect on him. He reacts adversely to overdemanding supervision and overdemanding jobs. The pursuit of a satisfying personal life sometimes takes precedence over his career objectives. Most important, he doesn't want to stay at *just* a job; he wants to stay at the *right* job.

COMMONSENSE ACTIONS

1. Managers who want to retain valued employees will have to pay attention to the "total person." When making decisions that may extend beyond the employee's work life, the manager will have to take into consideration relocation, travel, overtime, and emotionally demanding assignments that may affect the employee both at work and at home.

2. Participative management is a popular concept today. However, many managers give it only lip service. In the future, in the pursuit of a better quality of work life, employees will demand more participation in management as a basic condition of continued employment.

MATRIX ORGANIZATION

All the turnover problems discussed in this chapter place a strain on the traditional hierarchical organization. In the future, employees will be less willing to wait for an opening in a higher-level job to start performing responsible and satisfying work assignments. They will be less tolerant of status inequities inherent in the hierarchical system. They will demand the right to make a contribution according to ability rather than rank. They will refuse to be limited to the range of work assignments assigned by a job description.

COMMONSENSE ACTIONS

1. More and more companies are discovering that a matrix organization satisfies their current needs. This system provides greater flexibility to move people in and out of work assignments. Working in project teams with people from different disciplines, and reporting to more than one person, gives employees variety, challenge, and an opportunity for greater accomplishment.

2. The hierarchical system won't disappear. But progressive organizations, recognizing the difficulties in retaining a strong workforce, may adopt a combination of hierarchical matrix-type systems.

Throughout this book, I have emphasized turnover as a complex problem, symptomatic of underlying organizational problems. Most important, I have stressed that turnover should be everyone's concern, and that line managers are in a unique position to do something about it. By taking the commonsense actions described throughout the book—all of which are readily available and within their authority—managers can have a profound impact on reducing turnover.

Index